Preface

Everyone needs money, right? Everyone needs money since he/she were born to die, he/she need money, right?

The problem is that many people are hard to earn money to meet their daily needs. So how to deal with getting what you want.

Are you unemployed? Are you looking for a job? Are you in trouble for money? Need cash in a hurry? Of course, you do! Right?

If your answer is yes, then you need to read, study, and practice the contents of this book. After that, your fate will change. Ha...7x

Congratulations! Your financial problems can be overcome soon.

Richard Nata is the author of:
1. How to Create Great Articles for SEO in Three Hours.
2. The Best Way To Stop Watching Porn Today.
3. How to Skyrocket 7-8 Figure Income Annually from Blogging.
4. Want More Traffic? 514 Tips to Skyrocket Your Website Traffic and Income Faster.
5. How to Start a Business With China.
6. Why Do Trump and Some Other US Presidents Endorse a New World Order?
7. Knowing Jesus Better - the Real Jesus According to Thousands of Verses and Who is Jesus to you?
8. How to Win a Soul to Jesus Christ.
9. Top Secret of Healthy Life Revealed.
10. Top Secret of Longevity Revealed.
11. Top Secret of Healthy Life and Longevity Revealed.
12. Make Your First $5,000 Faster: How to Find and Get Your Perfect Job.

Thank you for reading and giving a good review for my book.
Lord Jesus blesses you. Amen.

Table of Contents

Preface 1
Table of Contents 2
Introduction 4
Kinds of Work Type 7
Determine Your Career Goals as a Full-Time Freelancer 10
Do Not Waste Your Time on Social Media 11
Focus 11
Choose a Freelance Job You Love 13
A Full-Time or Part-Time Job 15
A Full-Time Job or Full-Time Freelancer 16
Which Is Better a Full-Time Job or a Full-Time Freelancer? 18
Revenue Target 18
How to Get $5,000 Quickly as a Full-Time Freelancer 24
English as a Second Language (ESL) 25
Be Confident and Immediately Apply for a Freelance Job 26
Pray to God 27
Doing a Research 28
Active Income, Passive Income, or Both 30
How to Get Both, Active Income and Passive Income 32
Become a Freelancer 33
My Story as a Freelancer 34
How Online Freelance Work Has Impacted My Life 35
10 Ways to Get Jobs as a Freelancer 38
How to Find a Freelance Job Faster 39
Create a Great Cover Letter 41
Examples of the Great Cover Letters 43
Create a Great Resume 48
Example of a Great Resume 49
Make Your Cover Letter and Resume Become One Page 53
Use the Power of Words 54
Always Check and Recheck 55
14 Simple Ways to Attract the Client's Attention 56
21 Golden Rules of Seeking a Freelance Job 57
Bid Strategy 59

How to Make Your Client Impressed While Reading Your Bid 60
Examples of the Winning Bids 60
Test Online 66
Interview through Chat, Email, or Video Call 67
Lessons Learned: What a Lost Test and Interview Really Tells You 68
Why Didn't You Get a Freelance Job There? 69
201 Amazing Ways to Make Your First $5,000 Faster 70
Become a Writer 76
Become a Freelance Writer 81
Become an Author 84
Become a Novelist 88
Become a Ghostwriter 93
Become a Blogger 94
Become a Website Manager 98
Become a Content Creator 98
Become an SEO Writer 99
Become an Editor/Proofreader 100
Become an Entrepreneur 100
Become a Business Plan Writer 102
Become a Public Speaker 102
Become a Motivator 103
Become a Private Teacher 104
Become an Online Teacher 104
Become a Translator 105
Become an Interpreter 105
Become a Journalist/Reporter 106
Become a Nanny 106
Become a Baby Sitter 107
Become a Pet Sitter 107
Become a Dog Trainer 108
Become a Pet Grooming 108
Become an Animal Breeder 109
Animal Care Services 109
Become a Gardener 109
Become an Entertainer 110
Become a Programmer 110

Become a Fashion Designer 111
Become a Graphic Designer 112
Become a Jewelry Designer 113
Become a Painter 113
Become a Photographer 114
Become an Art Photographer 115
Become a Wedding Photographer 116
Become a Freelance Cameraman 116
Become a YouTuber 117
Creating Video Services 118
Make Video Subtitling 119
Make Video/Audio Transcript 120
Gift Wrapping Services 120
Sell the Secondhand Stuff 121
Online Shop 121
Culinary Business 122
Become a Virtual Assistant 122
Marketing Services in Social Media 123
Become a Buzzer 123
DIY souvenirs 124
Become a Singer 124
Conclusion 125

Introduction

Always think digital be global.

Most people dream of living their lives with freedom and passion, doing what they love, then they can finally relax and enjoy life, right?

Before you can get all the dreams above, then you should be able to make your first $5,000, right? So you should make your first $5,000 faster. After that, you will make your own destiny!

If you want to make your first $5,000 (and who doesn't, right?), see if this book is right for you.

This book is the knowledge you've been waiting for a long time. Because this book can show you a **faster**, **easier**, more **stress-free** and enjoyable way to get your first $5,000.

Read, study, and practice to it. Grab your first $5,000. And make something happen to you.

Believe it or not, you can get your first $5,000 faster because it works fine for us.

Do you really understand your passion and motivation to get your first $5,000? If yes, getting your first $5,000 is actually not hard since you know the secret. You will know the tactics to make your first $5,000 faster if you continue to read this book.

If you follow the step by step of this book, then your next step to make your first $5,000 is perfectly clear.

Do not be discouraged if you find this hard to do at first (I know, I did!). Keep practicing and it will become easier day by day.

I believe it is your time to make your first $5,000 now. Because this book not only gives theory but gives you guidance to get your first $5,000 faster.

What will you get on this book? Almost everything that makes your first $5,000 faster. So you started to think about how you could make that happen.

Everything you need to know to:
1. You started to think about how you could make your first $5,000 faster.
2. Learn and practice a method for making your first $5,000 with confidence & ease.

3. Looking for a job or freelance job.
4. Research.
5. You can make your first $5,000 faster.
6. Make a Great Cover Letter.
7. Make a Great Resume.
8. Past the interview successfully.
9. And many more.

Remember this!

Making your first $5,000 can be a long process. So you need to put more passion, time, and find the motivation to keep making money. If you can do it, then you've managed to speed up the process to get your first $5,000, right?

> Tony Robbins: "If you want to be successful, find someone
> who has achieved results you want
> and copy what they do..."

Richard Nata: Be patient. Success like running a marathon takes a long time. Today is the time for you to change. So just do it and never limit yourself. Then it is not you who pursue success, but success will catch you.

I have been young, and [now] am old; yet have I not seen the righteous forsaken, nor his seed begging bread (Psalms 37:25).

The blessing of the LORD, it maketh rich, and he addeth no sorrow with it (Proverbs 10:22).

Psalms {127:1} Except the LORD build the house, they labour in vain that build it: except the LORD keep the city, the watchman waketh [but] in vain. {127:2} [It is] vain for you to rise up early, to sit up late, to eat the bread of sorrows: [for] so he giveth his beloved sleep.

If you believe the above verses, then you do not have to worry anymore.

You have to work if you want to earn money, right.

If you can earn money without working, then you have turned your life into a beggar, or a robber, or a swindler.

For even when we were with you, this we commanded you, that if any would not work, neither should he eat (2 Thessalonians 3:10).

This book will take your life to a whole new level. For the person who's committed, anything is possible.

Psalms {1:1} Blessed [is] the man that walketh not in the counsel of the ungodly, nor standeth in the way of sinners, nor sitteth in the seat of the scornful. {1:2} But his delight [is] in the law of the LORD; and in his law doth he meditate day and night. {1:3} And he shall be like a tree planted by the rivers of water, that bringeth forth his fruit in his season; his leaf also shall not wither; and whatsoever he doeth shall prosper.

This book does not teach you to Get-rich-quick schemes, but teach you, how to get your first $5,000 faster as a full-time freelancer. After that, you can do it again and again and again. He...7x

So you better figure out how to get your work out there on a bigger scale and make money doing it.

The author believes, if you trust in God, work really hard, and you are kind, amazing things will happen.

Kinds of Work Type

According to Payable.com, a work type is a unit that determines what or how a worker is paid. Payable can accommodate any kind of work or method that you might use to calculate contractor compensation. This can be any common way to pay independent contractors such as Hourly, by the Project, Day Rate, etc. Or something more specific, like Photographs, Deliveries, Articles, or anything another unit of measuring the output of your contractors.

Basically, a work type is divided into:
1. Full-time job. The job takes a lot of your time, you usually work from 9 am to 5 pm. You usually work from Monday to Friday.

Payments are made once a week or month.

Full-time employment often comes with benefits that are not typically offered to part-time, temporary, or flexible workers, such as annual leave, sick leave, and health insurance.

If you can get a high position, then you usually get an annual bonus when the company gets a profit beyond the target set.

2. Part-time job. The job takes the fewer hours per week than a full-time job. You are not required to work from Monday to Friday. So your working hours are flexible.

Payments are made once a week/month based on the targets or commissions reached or after the work is done.

Part-time employment does not get annual leave, sick leave, health insurance, and annual bonus.

A part-time worker is also called a freelancer.

Your income as a freelancer depends on how active you are working because the more active you are, the more money you will make.

Besides full-time job and the part-time job, there are some terms you should understand.
1. Contract Job. A contract is an agreement among employee and employer setting out inferred, and implicit terms and conditions.

Employees and employers must stick to a contract until it ends or until the terms are changed.

2. Remote job or Anywhere. A remote job is one that is done away from the office in a remote location. This could be either work did from home or work is done on the road for a job such as a Regional Salesperson.

3. Telework Job or Telecommuting.
A telecommuting job sometimes called teleworking, is one where you trade your commute for a home-based job. Rather than traditional commuting, you are "commuting" by telephone and computer.

Most telecommuting jobs are done from home offices, but they may be part-time or full-time telecommuting jobs, meaning that the company may want you to be in the office for meetings or occasional face-time.

4. Home-Based Job.
This is perhaps the most obvious of all the remote job phrases here. Home-based jobs are those that you do from your home. This is also very similar to a virtual job because, usually, a job that is called home-based will be 100% done from your home without regular trips into the office for meetings and face-time.

Resource: https://www.flexjobs.com/blog/post/what-is-a-remote-job/

Of course, when applying for a job, you should check the job description to make sure that this is the kind of job you want. Therefore, you should do some research before you apply for a job.

Determine Your Career Goals as a Full-Time Freelancer

You must be serious about your career goals as a full-time freelancer because your future is determined by the plan you are creating now.

The first thing you should do is figure out your career goals as a full-time freelancer. Define success on your own terms and conditions. Then imagining where you want to be in a set several years.

How much time can you take your position to the next level?
What would be your dream position in the next year?
What would be your dream position in the next five years?
What would be your dream position in the next ten years?
What would be your dream position in the next 25 years?

Remember this! You should set some targets to reach in your career plan as a full-time freelancer.

Then you can write it down on a list.

Write down a list of your main strengths, weaknesses, personality type, skills, abilities, hobbies, and education.

Do not forget to write down, some abilities you want to improve in the future. If you need a degree for your dream role, plan how to get an appropriate degree in the next few years.

You have to believe in yourself. Do what you want. And be cool with it.

Do Not Waste Your Time on Social Media

Do not waste your time on social media.

Note this well. Many people who have spent hours each day to open Facebook, YouTube, Google+, Reddit, Instagram, StumbleUpon, Pinterest, Twitter, etc. And they do not make money at all.

Your time is limited, so don't waste it.

Time is influencing your future. Remember that "time is money" or more precisely to say if you can use your time well, then you will make more money. So, don't spend your valuable time on social media that don't bring you money.

Absolutely, you should make social media to promote your skill, ability, knowledge, experience, and portfolio. But you do not use for things that do not need such as chat, make comments on various posts, and debating any topic.

Steve Jobs said, "Your time is limited, so don't waste it living someone else's life."

Focus

When you are looking for a freelance job, then you have to focus on one or more particular field. To get a freelance job faster, then focus on areas that you like the most. And never turned your attention to other fields.

By focusing, you can quickly find out all the constraints, challenges, and problems while applying for a freelance job. The more focused you are, the faster you can get a freelance job. Stay focused on the creative process. And never lose the vision of your creative process.

The problem is that you often find it difficult to focus, right?

Remember this!
The focus is very important for achieving success! So you can focus on the real tactics and strategies. It's mostly about the things you do, not about how you feel.

Some things that distract your focus is:
1. A beep from the telephone, SMS (Short Message Service), or WA (Whatsapp). So turn off your smartphone.
2. Check email, LinkedIn, Facebook, Reddit, and other social media. Specify the time when you open the email, Facebook, Reddit, and other social media. Never open it other than the specified time, except your email. Because you should often check your email to see if there are companies that reply to your freelance job application.
3. TV and Video. So turn off your TV and DVD (Digital Video Disc).
4. Games. So turn off your games.

5. Hang out. Some friends may invite you to hang out. Reject them because you are now focused on finding a freelance job.

You are not working now. But you can focus on using the time from 9 am to 5 pm to find a freelance job.

Boring? Obviously very boring. But you can get a freelance job faster if you focus on doing this every day until you get a freelance job.

Remember this!

The faster you get a freelance job, the faster you get your first $5,000, right?

So, what are you waiting for?

Be focus and start looking for a freelance job.

Choose a Freelance Job You Love

Remember this!

You have to love your freelance job, love what you do, and do what you enjoy.

Don't settle for what other people want you to do, or what you think you should be doing — choose the freelance jobs that you are truly passionate about. So you can work on freelance jobs you are obsessed with. This is your perfect job.

Don't listen to those outside voices telling you what your work or career is "supposed" to look like. Do what you love, and focus on achieving what you set out to do. And do whatever you want. This is your perfect job.

Why should you choose the freelance job you love?

Confucius said, "Life is really simple, but we insist on making it complicated. Wherever you go, go with all your heart. It does not matter how slowly you go as long as you do not stop. Our greatest glory is not in never falling, but in rising every time we fall. Choose a job you love and you'll never work a single day in your life."

Steve Jobs said, "Your work is going to fill a large part of your life. And the only way to be truly satisfied is to do what you believe is great work. And the only way to do great work is to love what you do. If you haven't found it yet, keep looking. Don't settle. As with all matters of the heart, you'll know when you find it."

Richard Nata said, "A job that you love makes you know what you should do and do what you know. So, you just follow your passion and **make money living from your passion.** By doing that, the money will come by itself. After that, you can do whatever you want with the money you get. Because money can buy almost anything desired by people for life in this world."

If you do not spend your time to do what you like then you will easily become stressed if you have problems with your work. Right?

Richard Nata said, "Understanding why you really do what you love. If you really love your work, what you do is much more, have more energy, more fun, and more success. Right?"

So, what are you waiting for? You can set a freelance job target you believe in, a freelance job target you love now. This is your perfect job. ☺

After that, you can start applying for work at various companies that open vacancies in accordance with the field you love.

Richard Nata: If you want to succeed faster, then work with all your heart as you work for God.

Philippians {4:13} I can do all things through Christ which strengtheneth me.

Luke {16:10} He that is faithful in that which is least is faithful also in much: and he that is unjust in the least is unjust also in much.

Matthew {10:16} Behold, I send you forth as sheep in the midst of wolves: be ye therefore wise as serpents, and harmless as doves.

Colossians {3:23} And whatsoever ye do, do [it] heartily, as to the Lord, and not unto men;

Philippians {4:19} But my God shall supply all your need according to his riches in glory by Christ Jesus.

You can work in the profession you enjoy and obsessed with. Then the freelance job satisfaction and promotion will become your friend. This is your perfect job.

Don't forget to become a full-time freelancer to get your first $5,000 faster.

A Full-Time or Part-Time Job

Most people want to work full-time compared to part-time. Because, if they can work full-time, then their salary is paid every month. They get annual leave, sick leave, and health insurance. In addition, they will get various perks, facilities, and bonuses from the company.

Usually, the full-time job salary earned is higher compared to part-time job workers.

Is it true that a full-time job provides a better income than a part-time job? Absolutely right.

Therefore, you should look for a full-time job compared to a part-time job.

Why is that? Because a full-time job has more hours than a part-time job.

The question now is as follows. What if both have the same number of working hours or working hours of a part-time job is more than the working hours of a full-time job? Are the earnings in a full-time job greater than a part-time job?

The answer is not necessarily. The answer depends on your diligence, skill, knowledge, ability, and rate.

Why is that?

Read on in this book to get the answer.

A Full-Time Job VS Full-Time Freelancer

If you are working on two or more part-time jobs at once in the same or adjacent time, then you are said to be a full-time freelancer.

Although you work part-time, you can get more income if you are skilled and diligent in finding new jobs.

Examples are as follow.

1. You work as a Staff Writer. Your monthly salary is $3,000. You can complete 3 articles every day. Then you can earn $3,000 a month. For how many articles you make, your salary remains $3,000.

You work as a Freelance Writer. You get paid $50 per article. You can complete 3 articles every day or 90 articles a month. Then you can earn $4,500 a month.

2. You work as a Staff Programmer. Your monthly salary is $5,000. You can complete 2 websites a month. Then you can earn $5,000 a month. For how many websites you make, your salary remains $5,000.

You work as a Freelance Programmer. You get paid $3,000 per website. You can complete 2 websites a month. Then you can earn $6,000 a month.

The question now is why you can get more income if you become a full-time freelancer? The answer is if you work for a company then all the profits earned will belong to the company. And you only get paid with a fixed salary plus a bonus if any. Whereas, if you work as a full-time freelancer, then all the profits will be yours.

So a full-time job or full-time freelancer? Your decision will affect you, on your family, and on your career.

The author has worked as a full-time job in the office. The author also has worked as a full-time freelancer at home. Therefore, the author can say about the things below.

Which Is Better a Full-Time Job or a Full-Time Freelancer?

The answer is not necessarily. The answer depends on your diligence, skill, ability, knowledge, and rate.

The author's suggestion is that if you are just working for the first time, then you should find a job as a full-timer in a company. When working, you should improve your skills, ability, and knowledge, so you become an expert in your field of work.

After becoming an expert, you can start looking for freelance work in your field of work. After getting a lot of the repeat clients, then you resign from your job and become a full-time freelancer.

Why is that? Because you will get more income. In addition, you are free to work without having to be managed by a manager and/or boss. Right? Ha...7x

Do you agree with my suggestion? Or you have another strategy. It's up to you. Because this is your life. So you have to decide what you will do to earn money.

You can seek advice from your parents, wife/husband, friends, or neighbors before deciding whether you will be working a full-time job or full-time freelancer.

Revenue Target

The target revenue that the author sets out in this book is $5,000.

Of course, you can create your own target revenue. The more your target revenue, the better.

The example is:

1. Your revenue targeted $10,000.

2. Your revenue targeted $20,000.

You should really understand with your passion and motivation to get your first $5,000.

The target $5,000 is small for some people. But target $5,000 is big for some other people.

2018 Federal and State Minimum Wage Rates per Hour:

1. Alabama: $7.25 (Federal Minimum Wage, no state minimum).
2. Alaska: $9.84 (Annual indexing has begun).
3. Arizona: $10.50 (Raised to $12.00 through Indexed Annual Increases between 1/1/2019 to 1/1/2020).
4. Arkansas: $8.50.
5. California: $11.00 ($11.00 to $15.00 in $1.00 Indexed Annual Increases between 1/1/2019 to 1/1/2022).
6. Colorado: $10.20* ($10.20 to $12.00 in $0.90 Indexed Annual Increases between 1/1/2019 and 1/1/2020).
7. Connecticut: $10.10.
8. Delaware: $8.25.
9. District of Columbia: $12.50 (Increases to $15 with Indexed Annual Increases between 7/1/2018 and 7/1/2020).
10. Florida: $8.25*
11. Georgia: $5.15 if not covered by Federal Regulations otherwise $7.25 (Federal Minimum Wage).
12. Guam: $8.25.
13. Hawaii: $10.10.

14. Idaho: $7.25.
15. Illinois: $8.25.
16. Indiana: $7.25.
17. Iowa: $7.25.
18. Kansas: $7.25.
19. Kentucky: $7.25.
20. Louisiana: $7.25 (Federal Minimum Wage, no state minimum).
21. Maine: $10.00 (11.00 to $12.00 in $1.00 annual Increases between 1/1/2019 to 1/1/2020) (Indexed annual increases will begin on 1/1/2021).
22. Maryland: $10.10.
23. Massachusetts: $11.00 ($3.75 for tipped employees).
24. Michigan: $9.25 (Indexed annual increases will begin on 4/1/2019).
25. Minnesota: Large employers are required to pay workers $9.65/hour and small employers (less than 500k in annual sales) $7.87 (Indexed Annual increases will begin on 1/1/2018).
26. Mississippi: $7.25 (Federal Minimum Wage, no state minimum).
27. Missouri: $7.85.
28. Montana: $8.30 ($4.00 for businesses with gross annual sales of $110,000 or less) (Annual indexing has begun).
29. Nebraska: $9.00.
30. Nevada: $8.25 Nevada's minimum wage is set at $1.00 above the federal minimum wage for firms not providing health insurance.
31. New Hampshire: $7.25 (Federal Minimum Wage).
32. New Jersey: $8.60 (Annual indexing has begun).
33. New Mexico: $7.50.
34. New York: $10.40 ($0.70 Indexed Annual Increases from 12/31/2018 to $12.50 by 12/31/2020. Starting 1/1/2021, the rate will be adjusted annually for inflation until it reaches

$15 an hour) - More information on New York minimum wage increases.
35. North Carolina: $7.25.
36. North Dakota: $7.25.
37. Ohio: $8.30 ($7:25 for employers with gross sales of $283,000 or less) (Annual indexing has begun).
38. Oklahoma: $7.25.
39. Oregon: $10.75 (From $10.75 to $13.50 from 7/1/2019 to 7/1/2022).
40. Pennsylvania: $7.25.
41. Puerto Rico: $7.25.
42. Rhode Island: $10.10.
43. South Carolina: $7.25 (Federal Minimum Wage, no state minimum).
44. South Dakota: $8.65 (Annual indexing has begun).
45. Tennessee: $7.25 (Federal Minimum Wage, no state minimum).
46. Texas: $7.25.
47. Utah: $7.25.
48. Vermont: $10.50, Annual indexing begins 1/1/2019.
49. Virgin Islands: $9.50, $10.50, 6/1/18.
50. Virginia: $7.25.
51. Washington: $11.50 (From $12.50 to $13.50 from 1/1/2019-1/1/2020).
52. West Virginia: $8.75.
53. Wisconsin: $7.25.
54. Wyoming: $7.25, $5.15 if federal regulations do not apply.

According to the Economic Policy Institute, 40 localities have adopted minimum wages above their state minimum wage:

Albuquerque, New Mexico; Berkeley, California; Bernalillo County, New Mexico; Birmingham, Alabama; Chicago, Illinois; Cook County, Illinois; Cupertino, California; El Cerrito, California; Emeryville, California; Flagstaff, Arizona; Las Cruces, New Mexico; Los Altos, California; Los Angeles County, California; Los Angeles, California;

Malibu, California; Milpitas, California; Montgomery County, Maryland; Mountain View, California; Nassau, Suffolk, and Westchester Counties, New York; New York City, New York; Oakland, California; Palo Alto, California; Pasadena, California; Portland Urban Growth Boundary, Oregon; Portland, Maine; Prince George's County, Maryland; Richmond, California; San Diego, California; San Francisco, California; San Jose, California; San Leandro, California; San Mateo, California; Santa Clara, California; Santa Fe City, New Mexico; Santa Fe County, New Mexico; Santa Monica, California; SeaTac, Washington; Seattle, Washington; Sunnyvale, California; and Tacoma, Washington.

Data source: https://www.thebalancecareers.com/2017-federal-state-minimum-wage-rates-2061043

Top 10 national minimum wages **per Hour** 2015 in the world:

Australia $9.54.

Luxembourg $9.24.

Belgium $8.57.

Ireland $8.46.

France $8.24.

Netherlands $8.2.

New Zealand $7.55.

Germany $7.19.

Canada $7.18.

United Kingdom $7.06.

Data source: http://money.cnn.com/interactive/economy/top-10-national-minimum-wages-in-the-world/index.html

Working hours: 9 am – 5 pm or 8 hours.

Day hours: Monday – Friday or 5 days.

Week hours: 40 hours.

Bless you, if you live in the countries above because you only need 3 months or more to get your first $5,000.

15 Countries With The Cheapest Labor in 2017:

1. UGANDA - $0.01 per hour or $22 PER YEAR.
2. GEORGIA - $0.24 per hour or $96 PER YEAR.
3. CUBA - $0.05 per hour or $108 PER YEAR.
4. KYRGYZSTAN - $0.09 per hour, gets $14 per month or $181 PER YEAR.
5. BANGLADESH – $0.09 per hour, gets $19 per month or $228 PER YEAR.
6. TANZANIA - $0.1 per hour or $240 PER YEAR.
7. THE GAMBIA - $0.13 per hour or $317 PER YEAR.
8. VENEZUELA - $0.17 per hour or $361 PER YEAR.
9. GUINEA-BISSAU - $0.17 per hour or $372 PER YEAR.
10. MALAWI - $0.17 per hour or $412 PER YEAR.
11. LIBERIA - $0.17 per hour or $435 PER YEAR.
12. THE DEMOCRATIC REPUBLIC OF THE CONGO - $0.2 per hour or $472 PER YEAR.
13. TAJIKISTAN - $0.23 per hour or $487 PER YEAR.
14. GHANA - $0.23 per hour or $488 PER YEAR.
15. MADAGASCAR - $0.23 per hour or $490 PER YEAR.

Data source: https://www.therichest.com/world-money/15-countries-with-the-cheapest-labor/

If you live in the 15 countries above, then you need ten years or more to get your first $5,000.

Do not be too sad. Because this book will teach you how to earn $5,000 faster as a full-time freelancer.

How to Get $5,000 Quickly as a Full-Time Freelancer

Here are some things you should do so you can get $5,000 quickly as a full-time freelancer:

1. Pray to God.
2. Improve your English skills so you can read and write in English.
3. Doing a research.
4. **Start applying for work online**. Because it does not cost you anything, except the cost of using the internet. He...7x
5. Become the members of several job search sites like Indeed, Simple Hired, Upwork, Freelancer, Guru, FlexJobs, etc.
6. If your skills are writing, then you can apply through the websites that provide premium payment likes Problogger, IZEA, ClearVoice, CloudPeeps, Express Writers, etc.
7. Send your "Cover Letters + Resume" as much as possible every day.
8. Send your bid as much as possible every day.
9. Never stop sending your "Cover Letters + Resume" even if you've been interviewed. Because you may not get the job.
10. Never stop sending your bid even if you've been interviewed. Because you may not get the job.
11. Never stop sending "Cover Letters + Resume" and bid until you are get one or more the freelance job.

12. The most important thing is that you can start working as much as you can. So do not stop sending "Cover Letters + Resume" and bid, although you get a freelance job.
13. You can submit a job that you get to another freelancer if you can not do all the work yourself.
14. Increase your skill and ability.
15. Be smart and intelligent.
16. Be the master in your field.
17. Be helpful to your client.
18. Building trust.
19. Plan your future as a full-time freelancer.

English as a Second Language (ESL)

"Stay afraid, but do it anyway. What's important is the action. You don't have to wait to be confident. Just do it and eventually, the confidence will follow" – Carrie Fisher.

Bless you, if English is your native language. You will not have the difficulty in finding freelance jobs on various international websites.

Conversely, if English is not your native language, then you should be able to speak English first before you look for the freelance jobs on various international websites.

If your English is fluent, then you already have three skills as a translator or interpreter or Video/Audio Transcript.

Remember this!

If you want to make your first $5,000 faster, then think digital, be global.

Look for online jobs that you can do at home.

You can search for remote jobs and/or contract jobs. You can even search for one or more freelance jobs at once.

Be Confident and Immediately Apply for a Freelance Job

Many people are afraid to apply for work on various international websites because they think that their English is not good.

In fact, they are afraid of their own. Because who knows and who cares if your English is not good? Right?

To be honest, the English by the author is also mediocre. But the author is always confident to apply for work or make a bid on various international websites.

Why does the author dare to do that? The author dares to do it because the author has several strategies to overcome this problem.

There are four reasons why the author dares to do that:

1. There are many tools that make it easy for us to work. Currently, much software or tools translator from English to your language or vice versa. An example is we can use Google to translate online. Of course, Google translate is not accurate, so there are many mistakes when it translates a sentence.

2. The lack of Google translate can be covered with tools that can check for grammar, spelling, and typo errors. So this tool can do proofreading for you. There are many tools that you can use, either free or paid.
3. Besides tools, you can also use the services of someone to do editing and proofreading. You pay according to his/her expertise. The more expert the more expensive the price of the service you have to pay.
4. You can find a freelancer to do the tasks assigned to you. Of course, you pay for a cheaper price. An example is you get a gig to create two articles for $25 per article. Then you look for a freelancer who wants to work on the gig at a price of $10 per article. If successful, then you will earn a profit of $15 per article or $30 per gig.

You can do it too if you know how to overcome your shortcomings in English.

In facts, some famous bloggers in their articles often have errors in grammar, spelling, and typo. So do not ever be afraid to make mistakes in writing. Right? Ha...7x

Pray to God

Always involve God in your plans. Ask God's direction and wisdom!

Pray that God will always intervene so that you can get the freelance job quickly.

Romans {8:28} And we know that all things work together for good to them that love God, to them who are the called according to [his] purpose.

Philippians {4:13} I can do all things through Christ which strengtheneth me.

Philippians {4:19} But my God shall supply all your need according to his riches in glory by Christ Jesus. {4:20} Now unto God and our Father [be] glory for ever and ever. Amen.

If you do not mind, then you can pray to the Lord Jesus. For Jesus is the Lord of the heavens and the earth.

You can see the evidence that Jesus is the creator of the universe and man through my book entitled "Top Secret of Healthy Life and Longevity Revealed."

If you want, then you can pray like this.

Father in the name of Jesus. Today I came to You to ask for Your help. I'm looking for the freelance jobs to earn $5,000 as soon as possible.

After earning $5,000, I hope You will multiply it so I will not be short of money anymore.

You have promised to ask for anything in Your name, then we will accept it. So I now ask for the freelance jobs to earn $5,000 as soon as possible and I definitely accept it.

Thank you, Jesus.

Amen.

Doing Research

Remember this!

Research is one of the most important things in making money.

Use these questions when you were doing research:

a. Why do you have to start looking for a freelance job?
b. What are the skill, knowledge, experience, and ability you want to offer to the company or client?
c. Do your skill, knowledge, experience, and ability match what the company or client requested?
d. What is your strategy for finding a freelance job?
e. What salary or rate do you ask?
f. When can you get a freelance job?
g. Etc.

You must read carefully the various requirements that are requested by the company or client. Can you fulfill it?

You must find out what the company or client wants, then give it to them.

You can know what the company or client wants by looking at the job specification given in the job vacancy. If you can meet all the specifications the company or client requested, then you can send "a Cover Letter + Resume" or bid it.

If you cannot meet all the specifications the company or client requested, then you cannot send "a Cover Letter + Resume" or bid it. Because it is wasting your time. Unless you can offer better to them.

Example:
JA offers a "link building for SEO" job to increase the ranking of his website.

The author offers the services of making the desired keyword is on page 1 of Google with a 100% money back guarantee if it does not work.

Then the author gets a job, which is actually not the expertise of the author (link building). Because he offers better than requested by JA.

Active Income, Passive Income, or Both

Sometimes success takes a long time. Take your time and choose those you can work with for a long time. The key is to pay attention to all the details and keep working your plan until you reach the goals you've set for yourself.

Currently, there are two types of income that is active income and passive income.

Active income is where you get paid for what you do. If you work in an office or do freelance work for clients, then your income is named as an active income.

Passive income is:
1. You do a job once, but you get paid many times. So you get income based on what is generated from the work you are doing now.
2. Work towards something that doesn't just end if you decide to take some time off.
3. Working hard today creates something that will work hard for you tomorrow.

The examples of passive income are you can create a book/eBook, program for gameplay, or app. You just make it once. And since the book/eBook or game or app is sold then you continue to earn income every month.

Besides making books/eBooks, software programs, apps, passive income can also be obtained from advertising on blogs, affiliate marketing, renting your home, deposits, buying stock to get an annual dividend, mutual funds, bonds, investing in a startup, etc.

Passive income seems easy and fun, but to get it is not easy. Often you have to spend a lot of time and/or spend a lot of money for investment. Or you do both, then you can get passive income in the large numbers.

If you want the passive income from advertising on blogs and affiliate marketing, then you should be able to attract to tens of thousands of people, hundreds of thousands, or millions of people, then you can get a big income. If you are not attracting tens of thousands of people, hundreds of thousands, or millions of people, then you can get a few dollars to teens dollars. Right?

If you are making books/eBooks, software programs, or apps, then you should sell for tens of thousands of people, hundreds of thousands, millions of people, or you only can get a few dollars to teens dollars. Right?

If you are renting your home, buying stocks to get an annual dividend, deposits, mutual funds, bonds, investing in a startup, then you must have big capital. If there is no capital, then you cannot get the high passive income. Right?

If people are told to choose between active income and passive income, of course, most people will choose both. Right? Ha...7x

The question now is whether you can get both? Of course, can get both active income and passive income at the same time.

How to Get Both, Active Income and Passive Income

You can get active income and passive income at the same time if you know how to get it.

The trick is as follows:
1. You work to earn active income. A portion of your income is set aside for savings. Once your savings are enough, you can invest in stocks, deposits, or mutual funds to earn passive income.
2. You can take the time to write a book. Once finished, the book can be offered to a large publisher or you publish it yourself to get the passive income.
3. You can also pay a ghostwriter to write a book. Once finished, the book can be offered to a large publisher or you publish it yourself to get passive income. You can sell your book in format eBook and paperback to get maximum results.
4. You must say that making a paperback book should spend a lot of money, right? You are wrong. Amazon KDP (Kindle Direct Publishing) gives you the opportunity to publish your book in paperback format for free now. This is the fact wrote on the Amazon website. You can now publish paperback versions of your books with KDP.
5. You can pay a programmer to make a game or an app. Once finished, you can sell it online via Google Play or Apple Store.

6. You can also give your game or app for free. Anyone can use or play it. You advertise in the game or app so you can get passive income
7. Etc.

Become a Freelancer

Become a freelancer is a fast, free, and way easier to get a job than getting a full-time job.

Being a freelancer means that you work part-time. So you are not bound by time 9 to 5 work hours. But this is one of the best jobs for people who are not working and/or students.

If you want to earn more money than you should be a full-time freelancer.
Here's a list of websites that use part-time workers:
1. There are thousands of job opportunities every day here: Freelancer.com, Upwork.com (formerly oDesk), Elance.com (In 2015 Upwork.com has acquired Elance.com), Guru.com, FlexJobs, etc.
2. Get paid to write via Textbroker.
3. Get paid to write product reviews: Dooyoo.
4. Get paid to write music reviews: Slicethepie.
5. Surveys: GlobalTestMarket, MOBROG, InboxDollars, Pinecone Research, Swagbucks.
6. Get paid to search online via Qmee.
7. Get paid to watch video through Maximiles, Gift Hunter Club, Gift Hulk.
8. Get paid to read adverts on your smartphone via Qustodian.
9. Get paid to click ads and/or read ads: NeoBux, ClickSense, Traffic Monsson, paidverts, etc.

10. Earn money with micro jobs: Clickworker, Field Agent, Amazon's Mechanical Turk, TaskRabbit.
11. Get paid to binge-watch movies and shows on Netflix.

All you have to do as a freelancer is show your skill, ability, knowledge, and experience to your clients. So they can see that you're the perfect person to get their job done, exactly the way they want it.

Offer detailed descriptions of what the client actually wants; the more you know, the better. After that, give it what they want.

In the freelance jobs, the clients did not ask about your background, education, training, or anything else, because they really do not care about it. Ha ... 7x

What they care about is that they pay you to complete the work they provide with good results and satisfy them. Ha ... 7x

3 Freelance Economy Success Stories.
https://www.forbes.com/sites/tjmccue/2013/06/28/3-freelance-economy-success-stories/
How to Make Money On Upwork – My $100,000 Year.
https://freelancetowin.com/how-to-make-money-on-elance-my-100k-year/

My Story as a Freelancer

This is my story. A true story.

I am always looking for better-paying gigs to increase my income. If I can, then you can certainly do it too. It worked for me, and it will work for you too.

Ask what they want, and convince them that you are the one who can get them there. *Ask if they're interested, how about you send them a proposal today? Then you can let them know if they want to do this.*

How Online Freelance Work Has Impacted My Life

I love to read and write. Being a professional writer makes my life more passion.

I'm an author, blogger, writer, novelist, ghostwriter, and SEO writer with specialist the first page of Google and/or Yahoo.

When reading articles on the internet, then I know that I can earn a lot of money from writing articles. Therefore, I started a blog in January 2015. In December 2015, I started to get a job to write an article for a client's website.

Since January 2016, I've got some clients. A few clients re-order the articles from me. When viewing the articles that I've made there are many which appear on the first page of Google and/or Yahoo, then I know that I was a writer who had a flair. I also realized that I was an SEO writer with the specialist the first page of Google and/or Yahoo.

In fact, many of my articles are become number 1 on Google.

Here's the proof:

1. An Article Get 24 number 1 & 53 Page 1 on Google. http://lifeonearthasinheaven.blogspot.co.id/2017/12/an-article-get-24-number-1-51-page-1-on_84.html.
2. The First Page of Google Ranking With Long-Tail Keywords or My Google+. http://lifeonearthasinheaven.blogspot.co.id/2016/02/the-first-page-of-google-ranking-with.html.
3. I Can Create the First Page of Google Ranking for $300 per Article. http://lifeonearthasinheaven.blogspot.co.id/2016/03/i-can-create-first-page-of-google.html.

Keywords:
Pintu otomatis - Number 1 on Google.
Pintu otomatis kaca - #1.
Cargo Impor Bangkok Jakarta - #1.
Impor Bangkok Jakarta - #1.
Jual artwork Jakarta - #1.
Jual artwork Indonesia - #1.
Jual artwork online - #1.
Token PLN - #1.

Since then, I started to offer SEO services to my clients. Services that I offer is, I can write articles that will make my client's website appear on the first page of Google and/or Yahoo. I even dare assure my clients that the website for my clients will surely appear on the first page of Google and/or Yahoo. If not successful, then I will give new articles free of charge to their website appears on the first page of Google and/or Yahoo.

The services I offer was getting a good response from my clients. So I've got a client who requested that their websites appear on the first page of Google and/or Yahoo. And I've managed to prove that their website appears on the first page of Google and/or Yahoo.

Here's a list of the services that I offer to the prospective clients:

1. The first page of Google and/or Yahoo
2. SEO Writing

3. Books/eBooks
4. Essay Writing
5. Articles Writing/Rewriting
6. Copy Writing
7. Creative Writing
8. Editing/Proofreading
9. Ghost Writing
10. Magazines and Newspapers-writing
11. Novel Writing
12. Websites/Blogs/Contents Writing
13. Short Stories Writing
14. Business Plan
15. Marketing
16. Slogans
17. Social Media
18. Translation: English – Indonesian and/or Indonesian – English

After getting a lot of clients, then I can say that my income is getting better from day to day because I have been several times tariff changes. My rates start at $2.5 per article, then $4, then $6, then $16, then $22, then $24, then $30, then $40, and then $50. A few months later became $60, $85, $100, and $180.

And now, I'm looking for clients who are willing to pay an additional $300 per article. :)

I trust and believe that my income will continue to increase every year.

If you want your website to appear on the first page of Google and/or Yahoo, then do not hesitate to contact me at richardnata0@gmail.com.

I guarantee you will be satisfied with the results of my articles for your website will appear on the first page of Google and/or Yahoo.

Thank you.

Lord Jesus blesses you.

Amen.

Remember this!

You can make more money as a full-time freelancer. The more active you are, the more money you'll make. And **don't expect overnight success as a full-time freelancer.**

10 Ways to Get Jobs as a Full-Time Freelancer

To get a freelance job is much easier than getting a full-time job.

10. Ways to Get Jobs as a full-time freelancer:

1. Apply for a freelance job as when applying for work in the office. How to apply by sending a Cover Letter + Resume.

You can read, study, and practice my book below.

Make Your First $5,000 Faster: How to Find and Get Your Perfect Job. https://www.amazon.com/dp/B07FVKQX8J.

2. Join or become a member of a marketplace that provides freelance jobs there. How to apply by sending a bid to the client.

3. Offer freelance services through your website and/or blog.

4. Put an ad in print or online media to offer your freelance services.

5. Offer your freelance services in the forums.

6. Offer your freelance services in social media like Facebook, Instagram, or Twitter.

7. Offer your freelance services to the companies and/or people who use your services. Send them via email.

8. Create brochures about your freelance services and then disseminate to your society or community.

9. You can look for a lot of clients. The more clients, the better.

10. You should get a lot of loyal clients. Because they can give you the repeat orders or jobs. The more loyal clients, the better.

How to Find a Freelance Job Faster

Almost all countries have several websites where you can search for the freelance jobs there.

Remember this!

1. Be digital and looking for at the global freelance jobs.
2. Browsing teens to hundreds of website that provide the freelance job vacancies every day.
3. Discipline. You should send hundreds of "Cover Letter and Resume" and/or bids every day.

Why? The more websites you browse, the more freelance job vacancies are available. And the more you submit your bids and/or "Cover Letter and Resume," the greater your chances of getting a freelance job.

If the more chance you get a freelance job, the faster you get a freelance job. Right?

So open all the websites that exist below. Find the freelance jobs that match your passion. Then, send your "Cover Letter and Resume" or bids to them.

List of websites that provide freelance job vacancies:

1. Indeed. www.indeed.com.
2. Dribbb. https://dribbble.com/
3. WayUp. https://www.wayup.com/.
4. TARGET Jobs. https://targetjobs.co.uk/
5. Jobs.ie. www.jobs.ie.
6. CAREERBUILDER. www.careerbuilder.com/
7. StartWire. https://www.startwire.com/
8. SimplyHired. http://www.simplyhired.com.
9. Glassdoor. https://www.glassdoor.com/
10. Flexjobs. https://www.flexjobs.com/
11. Jobrapido. Jobrapido.com
12. LinkedIn. https://www.linkedin.com/
13. MediaBistro. https://www.mediabistro.com/
14. JobDiagnosis.com. https://www.jobdiagnosis.com/
15. Craigslist. https://www.craigslist.org/
16. JobsRadar. www.jobsradar.com/
17. Jora. https://www.jora.com/
18. SnagAJob. https://www.snagajob.com.
19. Dice. https://www.dice.com.
20. Career Jet. https://www.careerjet.com/j
21. CareerBliss. https://www.careerbliss.com/
22. Etc.

Of course, there are still tens to hundreds of other websites that have not been mentioned above. You can do research through search engines.

They will send the freelance jobs available to you every day. The freelance vacancies are already selected in accordance with your selection/passion.

Remember this!

If you upload your Resume on various websites above, do not ever include your full address, ID card, Credit Card, or your family's name list. Do not let your personal data misused others.

Or you can search the freelance jobs through the marketplace websites that provide freelance job vacancies. After that, you can become a member there. And bids for the jobs you want.

Create a Great Cover Letter

If you want to get active income, then you have to get one job first. To get a job, then you must apply for work first. And to apply for work, then you must send Cover Letter/**Application Letter** and Resume/**Curriculum Vitae (CV)** first.

Remember this!

You have seconds to make a great first impression.

The first impression is very important. Your Cover Letter and Resume are a reflection of yourself, which is considered to represent your skill, ability, knowledge, experience, quality, and character. So make the client trust with your knowledge, ability, skill, experience, quality, and character!

Remember this too!

- Be Professional.
- Be Personal.
- Be specific.
- Keep it simple and smart (KISS).
- Use short sentences.
- Use short paragraphs.
- Show your worth.

You must have added value to win the competition through your Cover Letter and Resume. Because if you lose compete, then you will never be called for test and/or interview. And without a test and/or interview, you will never be able to work there.

So prepare your Cover Letter and Resume well. Because you have to win in the first competition, based on the Cover Letter and Resume you sent to the company or client.

Remember this!

Your Cover Letter and Resume are the first time assessed by the company or client when they are looking for an employee. So you should be able to attract the attention of a Human Resource Manager or client. Because if you cannot attract the attention of the Human Resource Manager or client, then your chances to work there gone with the wind. So you have to win here.

To win in the first competition, then you should be able to make a great Cover Letter and a great Resume first.

How to create a great Cover Letter:

1. Make an interesting design.
2. Make a great first impression.

3. Be Professional.
4. Be Personal.
5. Be nice.
6. Be unique.
7. Put your name in the first sentence.
8. Use the first person in your sentences.
9. Use the power words in your sentences. Power words are the words with emotion that make the audience become happy, sad, angry, sympathy, etc. Of course, the power words you choose are those that can give positive emotions to the client, boss and/or company.
10. Customize your Cover Letter for different jobs.
11. Show your knowledge, skill, ability, and experience.
12. Show your confidence.
13. Tell them what are the benefits of the client or company if they recruit you as their employee.
14. Keep it short.
15. Include your resume and photo.
16. Don't repeat your resume.
17. Address to Boss.
18. Send it online.
19. Close your Cover Letter with a call to action. Ask them to try you with a test and/or interview.

Examples of the Great Cover Letters

Here is an example that you can make a lesson or reference when writing a Cover Letter.

Of course, you do not need to copy and paste this example as you should be able to customize the example below to your needs.

Dear Boss,

I am the best fit for this job because:
1. I am an SEO specialist.
2. I am an author of 12 books on Amazon.

God gave the talent of writing fiction and nonfiction to me.

I have 22 years of working experience in writing. So I can give high-evergreen contents to you.

I can create your website on the first page of Google/Yahoo rankings with one article or more. Many of my articles are number 1 on Google and/or Yahoo.

The proof:
1. An Article Get 24 number 1 & 53 Page 1 on Google. http://lifeonearthasinheaven.blogspot.co.id/2017/12/an-article-get-24-number-1-51-page-1-on_84.html
2. The First Page of Google Ranking With Long-Tail Keywords or My Google+. http://lifeonearthasinheaven.blogspot.co.id/2016/02/the-first-page-of-google-ranking-with.html

Keywords:
Token PLN - Number 1 on Google.
Pintu otomatis - Number 1 on Google.
Pintu otomatis kaca - Number 1 on Google.
Cargo impor Bangkok Jakarta - Number 1 on Google.
Jual artwork Jakarta - Number 1 on Google.
Jual artwork Indonesia - Number 1 on Google.
Jual artwork online - Number 1 on Google.

My books on Amazon:
1. Want More Traffic? 514 Tips to Skyrocket Your Website Traffic and Income Faster. https://www.amazon.com/dp/B0778LTNQ1 - ebook.

https://www.amazon.com/dp/1973254514 - paperback.
2. How to Create A Great Article for SEO in Three Hours.
https://www.amazon.com/dp/B01M0I6WMH - ebook.
https://www.amazon.com/dp/1521169330 - paperback.
3. The Best Way To Stop Watching Porn Today.
https://www.amazon.com/dp/B075VCT82K - ebook.
https://www.amazon.com/dp/1549797530/ - paperback.
4. How to Skyrocket 7-8 Figure Income Annually from Blogging.
https://www.amazon.com/dp/B0765ZTCFX - ebook.
https://www.amazon.com/dp/1549901796 - paperback.
5. How to Start a Business With China.
https://www.amazon.com/dp/B078VHPLXV - ebook.
https://www.amazon.com/dp/1976826691/ - paperback.
6. Why Do Trump and Some Other US Presidents Endorse a New World Order?
https://www.amazon.com/dp/B078WNNWC5 - ebook.
https://www.amazon.com/dp/1976845351 - paperback.
7. Knowing Jesus Better - the Real Jesus According to Thousands of Verses and Who is Jesus to you? https://www.amazon.com/dp/B07BJDPR5Y - ebook.
https://www.amazon.com/dp/1980553998 - paperback.
8. How to Win a Soul to Jesus Christ.
https://www.amazon.com/dp/B07C1DQXYJ - ebook.
9. Top Secret of Healthy Life Revealed.
https://www.amazon.com/dp/B07D9T5FB8 - ebook.
https://www.amazon.com/dp/1982992212 - paperback.
10. Top Secret of Longevity Revealed.
https://www.amazon.com/dp/B07DDW91R7 - ebook.
https://www.amazon.com/dp/1983039896 - paperback.
11. Top Secret of Healthy Life and Longevity Revealed.
https://www.amazon.com/dp/B07DHNNVYX - ebook.
https://www.amazon.com/dp/1983064572 - paperback.
12. Make Your First $5,000 Faster: How to Find and Get Your Perfect Job.
https://www.amazon.com/dp/B07FVKQX8J - ebook.
https://www.amazon.com/dp/1717901123 - paperback.

Why should you hire me? I can make your business grow faster than you can imagine through my writings.

Questions and Answers:

1. In an ideal world, who are you writing for?
The audiences who want to read, study and practice the knowledge it gained from my articles or my books.
2. How much time do you dedicate to writing every day? 10 hours or more.
3. Who was your favorite client & why? Wira Cargo and Sepulsa. Because many of my articles are getting page 1 of Google and Yahoo.
4. How long will it take you to complete one article? 3-5 days.
5. How much do you expect to earn? $300 per article. Just for you, my rate $100.

Thank you for your review.
Lord Jesus blesses you.
Amen.

The example above is useful to you if you have had previous work experience.

What if you have never had previous work experience? Often you lose out in competing for the opportunity to work with those who have had work experience. Right? What will you do next?

Example of a great Cover Letter if you have never had previous work experience.

Dear Boss,

I am writing to apply for the position of a Clerk, which I saw advertised on Indeed.com. As a recent graduate of the XXX University, I have a significant background in Accounting. I believe that I am an ideal candidate for this position at your company.

Why me?

This is the reasons:

1. *Diligent.*
2. *Smart.*
3. *Dedicated.*
4. *Honest.*
5. *Thorough.*
6. *To be responsible.*
7. *Can be trusted.*
8. *Hard worker.*
9. *Ready to work overtime.*
10. *Always pay attention to details.*
11. *Can keep the company secrets.*

I am excited about the opportunity to join your team as a Clerk.

Try me and you will know that I do not lie to you.

Thank you for your time and consideration.

Sincerely,

Your Signature (hard copy letter)

Your Typed Name

Besides examples of Cover Letters in this book, you should also look at many examples that exist on the internet. After that, make a Cover Letter that bests suits you.

Remember this!

Always custom your Cover Letter because every job has different specifications.

Create a Great Resume

Prepare your resume well. Because you have to make a great Resume or **Curriculum Vitae (CV)**.

Everything listed on the Resume is relevant to the freelance job position.

You should create a great resume so **that makes you stand out from others. So show your worth. And impress your client.**

How to create a great resume:

1. Be creative and make an interesting design. Make it eye-catching.
2. Customize your Resume for different jobs.
3. Marketing yourself with your resume.
4. Positive attitude.
5. Professional mindset.
6. Be Personnel.
7. Put your name in the first sentence.
8. Use the first person in your sentences.
9. Use the power words in your sentences. Power words are the words with emotion that make the audience become happy, sad, angry, sympathy, etc. Of course, the power words you choose are those that can give positive emotions to the boss and/or company.
10. Put the position you are applying for.
11. Give your color photo.
12. Put your LinkedIn profile.
13. Put your social media profile.
14. Show your knowledge, skill, and experience.

15. Focus on your strengths.
16. Tell them what are the benefits of the client or company if they recruit you as their employee.
17. Keep it easy to read. Make sure the font is not too big or too small (choose a size between 10 and 12).
18. Don't repeat your cover letter.
19. Address to Boss.
20. Close your Resume with a call to action. Ask them to try you with a test and/or interview.
21. **Save your resume file as a PDF. Save with your name.**
22. Send it online.

Example of a Great Resume

Everything listed on the Resume is relevant to the freelance job position you are applying for.

The contents of your great resume:

1. Name.
2. The position you are applying for.
3. Address.
4. Phone and Skype.
5. Executive Profile.
6. Portfolio.
7. Work Experience.
8. Skill Highlights.
9. LinkedIn.
10. Blogs.
11. Social Media.
12. Interests.

13. Tagline.
14. Responsibilities.
15. Accomplishments.
16. References.
17. Education.

Remember this!

1. A one-page resume is sufficient. The client does not need to see your full-length resume, use the example to write one that's brief and to the point.
2. If a lot of data you want to convey then you can divide it into two or three columns in one page.
3. You must show your strength in your resume. Focus on your skills, ability, expertise, portfolio, work experience, and references. And never show your weakness to the client or company.
4. You may enter data from your hobbies and interests if it can add value. If not, then you do not need to provide your hobbies and interests in your resume.
5. Create a short, catchy statement that sells you and your skills. Show off your biggest achievements.
6. Add a sentence to bring attention to your value as a candidate. An example is "I am the best person to fill this position."
7. Show the client or company if you are the right person to fill the position offered. Then you give the reasons.
8. Challenge them with this sentence. Try me a month and you'll be surprised to see what I can do for the company.
9. Don't forget to make your resume unique. Create an interesting design.

10. Never copy-paste your resume for each job you apply for. Because each job offered has a different job description. So you have to adjust your resume to the specifications requested by the client or company.

Richard Nata

I am the author of 11 books on Amazon: Christianity – Business – Lifestyle – Fiction – Etc

I am a good SEO writer from Indonesia with the first-page of Google specialization.

An article from me made Wira Cargo rank #1 on Google through 24 keywords.

My rate: $300 per article (3,000 words or more)

Email: richardnata0@gmail.com – LinkedIn: https://www.linkedin.com/in/richard-nata-45002686/ – Blog: Life on Earth as in Heaven.

Executive Profile
I am an entrepreneur, consultant to Go Public (IPO) in Indonesia Stock Exchange, author, novelist, essayist, blogger, and ghostwriter. My articles, including short stories, published in Magazines and newspapers since 1994. I have written a lot of books, both fiction, and nonfiction. So, I was a professional in writing, both fiction, and non-fiction.

Professional Experience
In 1997, Richard Nata wrote a book entitled "Buku Pintar Mencari Kerja." This book is reprinted as much as 8 times. Through the book, the authors successfully helped tens of thousands of people get jobs at once successful in their careers. They were also successful when moving to work in other places.
Read more: http://richardnata.blogspot.com/2015/01/buku-pintar-mencari-kerja.html
Author – 1995 Until Now
Writer – 1994 Until Now
General Manager, TSP International Co. – Textile Stores – Resign 1994
Finance Manager, PT. Infopen – Export and Import – Resign 1992
Finance Supervisor, PT. Danamon Asuransi – Insurance – Resign 1990
Staff Accountant, PT. Indo Mobil Utama – Car Factory – Resign 1988

Technical Skills
Accounting – Finance – Management – Marketing – Social Media – Translation – Writing – SEO – Business Plan – Slogan – Short Story – Book/eBook – The First Page of Google – Creative Writing – Content Creator – Novel

Education
Atmajaya University with a honor degree in management – Graduated 1993

Tagline
Our expertise and services can solve your problems

Try me and you will be surprised to see the results

You'll have to modify it to fit your persona.

The example above is useful to you if you have had previous work experience.

What if you have never had previous work experience?

You can use the Resume above. But you should omit the data about the Professional Experience. Because you have no previous work experience.

Maybe you can write about your experience in organizing or your experience while working internship.

Make Your Cover Letter and Resume Become One Page

Remember this!

1. The higher the position in the company, the busier they are.
2. The bigger the company the busier the management.
3. Sharpen your Cover Letter and Resume.
4. Be Professional.
5. Be Personnel.
6. Be nice.
7. It would be nice if your Cover Letter and Resume are merged into one page so it does not take much time from the boss or client. Right?
8. One page of your data coupled with a good design will make your chances to get a job bigger. Right?
9. Your challenge to the boss or client will make you welcome to work there. Ha...7x

Source image: https://www.pexels.com/photo/graphs-job-laptop-papers-590016/

Use the Power of Words

Remember this!

You should always use the power of words to improve the emotions of your boss or client.

The more power of words you give, the better.

Always use the power of words on:

a. Your great Cover Letter.

b. Your great Resume.

c. Your bids.

Examples of the power of the word:

1. 150 Ways to Make Your First $5,000 – a good title.

150 Amazing Ways to Make Your First $5,000 Faster – a great title.

Amazing and faster are the power of words.

2. 50 Amazing Ways to Conquer Your Fear.

Amazing and conquer are the power of words.

3. The Best Way to Stop Watching Porn Today.

The best way and today are the power of words.

4. Mission: Impossible (a series of action spy films), Die Hard (movie), Spice Girls (English pop girl group), and Girl Power (Spice Girls popularized the slogan in the mid-1990s) are examples of the other power of words.

So you can start sprinkling your power words now. Because it will increase your chances of winning the competition to get a freelance job.

Always Check and Recheck

Things that can go wrong will go wrong. Never assume, but always check and verify. So always check and recheck twice or more.

You should edit and proofread twice or more before sending your bid or your Cover Letter and Resume.

Why? Because after reading over and over again, then you can see typos, spelling, or grammar errors. Or you can see the error based on sentence structure. You can fix it immediately.

14 Simple Ways to Attract the Client's Attention

Before you get a freelance job, then you should be tested and interviewed first. And to get tested and interview opportunities, then you should be able to attract the attention of the boss/client first.

How to communicate what makes you special to the client's say yes.

14 simple ways to attract the client's attention is:

1. Give your great Cover Letter.
2. Give your great Resume.
3. Give your great portfolio.
4. Show your strength, skill, ability, knowledge, and experience.
5. Be Professional.
6. Be Personnel.
7. Be nice.
8. Positive attitude.
9. Professional mindset.
10. Do not show your weaknesses.
11. Give your plan to the client.
12. Give your plan to the client's future.

13. Give many reasons why the client should choose you over the others.
14. Give the client a challenge to hire you.

21 Golden Rules of Seeking a Freelance Job

The author believes if you do the golden rule below, then you will get a freelance job quickly.

21 golden rules when looking for a freelance job:

1. Pray to God.
2. Doing a Research.
3. Talk less, do more.
4. Start making a great Cover Letter and Resume.
5. Start an email with the recipient's name or title. If you do not know, then replace it with the word "Boss." Because everyone likes to be called as boss.
6. Introduce yourself to one or two short sentences. You can write based on your perspective.
7. Give your photo in accordance with the company's dress code policy.
8. Don't forget to check and recheck your bids or your Cover Letter and Resume! Check for errors in data, typo, spelling, grammar, or sentence structure.
9. Never copy-paste your bids or your Cover Letter and Resume. You should customize your bids or your Cover Letter and Resume with the given the freelance job descriptions.
10. Send your bids or your Cover Letter and Resume every day. If necessary, send hundreds to thousands of

your Cover Letter and Resume every day until you get a freelance job.
11. Email should use your full name. Use richardnata0@gmail.com instead of rich123@gmail.com.
12. Your email should use Yahoo or Gmail.
13. Never stop applying for work until you get a freelance job. Because the rejection is part of looking for a freelance job. Almost every single employee has had a rejected when they're looking for a freelance job.
14. Never stop applying for work until you get a freelance job. Although you have been tested and interviewed at a company. Because you could have failed to work there for one reason or another.
15. Schedule your time to apply for a freelance job every day.
16. You need to set clear daily goals. An example is daily you send your Cover Letters and Resume to 250 companies and/or clients. Then stick to it.
17. If you join one or more marketplaces, then you can do several bids in each marketplace every day.
18. Use the flexibility. An example is you start opening job advertisements and apply for work from 9 am to 5 pm. But you can be flexible, apply for work at 7 am or 8 pm.
19. If you cannot get a freelance job, then you should create a job for yourself.
20. Ask for help from your parents, friends, family, or neighbors, so they would recommend you to the company, so you can get a freelance job faster.
21. Remove all your racist words on social media. Why? Because companies or clients sometimes do personnel background checks against their prospective employees.

Bid Strategy

Money is a sensitive issue for people. Therefore, the money you ask for when you bid will decide whether you can win a bid or not.

This is your dilemma.

If you ask too high, then you cannot compete with those who dare to be paid less. Conversely, if you ask too low, then you will be difficult to manage money for your routine needs every month.

Therefore, you must have a strategy when discussing the money you ask for your bid.

Here's your strategy:

1. Provide value in your bid. If possible, give more value than the client requested. Example. The client wants top 10 on Google. Give them top 5 on Google.
2. If you have never worked in the marketplace, then you should bid at the lowest bid limit. Because you should seek the work experience first. Besides, you are looking for clients who want to give 5 stars to you.
3. If you've worked before and got a few of 5 stars, then you can bid at the average of bid limit.
4. If you've worked before and got dozens of 5 stars, then you can bid at the highest bid limit.
5. If you want to win, then you can give a bonus to the client. Example. Give them money back guarantee.
6. If you get a lot of jobs then you can give a portion of the job you get to other freelancers if you can't do all the jobs that you get yourself.

How to Make Your Client Impressed While Reading Your Bid

As a freelancer, you must PROVE YOUR WORTH FIRST & PAY WILL GO UP DRASTICALLY.

Sometimes you can impress your client while reading your bid:

1. Show your worth and strength.
2. Show your knowledge, skill, ability, experience, and portfolio.
3. Give more value than the client requested.
4. Give one bonus or more to the client.
5. Give the money back guarantee to the client.

Examples of the Winning Bids

Examples of the bids that make the author got some freelance jobs:

1. Gig: Requires SEO improvement services on the website

Job details:

I Want to develop a service delivery business by increasing SEO on the website to appear on the first page on google search with some keywords as follows: services, delivery, import, wholesale, Guangzhou, China, Jakarta.

Thank you.

Regards.

Cover Letter.

Dear Boss,

With 1 million Rupiah, I will create 1-2 articles that will make your website a number 1 in Google and/or Yahoo rank with 1 keyword OR 2 POSITIONS ON THE FIRST PAGE OF GOOGLE AND/OR YAHOO. Because I am a specialist to be number 1 on Google and/or Yahoo rankings.

This is the proof:

Keyword: High traffic in one day then is number 1 in Google.

Another proof:

The First Page of Google Ranking With Long-Tail Keywords or My Google+.
http://lifeonearthasinheaven.blogspot.co.id/2016/02/the-first-page-of-google-ranking-with.html.

If my articles do not make your website a number 1 on Google and/or Yahoo OR 2 POSITIONS ON THE FIRST PAGE OF GOOGLE AND/OR YAHOO, then I will give you a new article for free to your website becomes number 1 on Google and/or Yahoo OR 2 POSITION ON THE FIRST PAGE OF GOOGLE AND/OR YAHOO.

Thank you.

The Lord Jesus blesses you.

Amen.

After several chats, the author gets the job.

2. Gig: Keyword optimization, link building, strategic content development.

Job details:

- Optimize keywords for website related to art products, for retail and B2B in Indonesia.

- Advice (may include execution) for the creation of content articles (content marketing) related to SEO plans, including the spread of links.

- Preferably living in Semarang to ease the necessary coordination meetings. However, there is no possibility of freelancers from other cities who can work remotely.

- A website, blog, and SEM basic already exist, some basic keywords already in the first search. Need to add the number of keywords and increase the ranking of existing keywords.

Cover Letter.

Dear Boss,

With 3 million Rupiah, then I will make your website on page 1 Google with 3 keywords.

The proof:

An Article Get 24 number 1 & 53 Page 1 on Google.
http://lifeonearthasinheaven.blogspot.co.id/2017/12/an-article-get-24-number-1-51-page-1-on_84.html.

Another proof:

The First Page of Google Ranking With Long-Tail Keywords or My Google+.
http://lifeonearthasinheaven.blogspot.co.id/2016/02/the-first-page-of-google-ranking-with.html.

Keyword:

CARGO IMPORT BANGKOK JAKARTA - number 1 in Google.

My books on Amazon:

1. Want More Traffic? 514 Tips to Skyrocket Your Website Traffic and Income Faster.
https://www.amazon.com.au/dp/B0778LTNQ1.

2. How to Start a Business With China.
https://www.amazon.com/dp/B078VHPLXV.

3. How to Create A Great Article for SEO in Three Hours.
https://www.amazon.com.au/dp/B01M0I6WMH.

4. Knowing Jesus Better - the Real Jesus According to Thousands of Verses and Who is Jesus to you?
https://www.amazon.com/dp/B07BJDPR5Y.

Thank you.

Lord Jesus blesses you.

Amen.

After several chats, the author gets the job.

3. Gig: Web SEO

Job details:

Requires specialist SEO.

Criteria:

1. Top 3 Google.

2. Three (3) Keywords.

Please mention the method that will be used and portfolio/web whoever done.

Cover Letter

Dear Boss,

If you want number 2 on Google and/or Yahoo, then the rate is 2 million Rupiah per keyword.

So 3 keywords: 6 million Rupiah.

The "Token PLN" keyword is numbered 1-2 on Google.

An article from me made Wira Cargo rank #1 on Google through 24 keywords.

The proof:

Do You Want to Be Number 1 on Google? Hire Richard Nata!

http://lifeonearthasinheaven.blogspot.co.id/2017/07/do-you-want-to-be-number-1-on-google.html.

My books on Amazon KDP.

How to Create A Great Article for SEO in Three Hours.

https://www.amazon.com/dp/1521169330?ref_=pe_870760_150889320 – paperback.

https://www.amazon.com/author/richardnata - ebook.

My latest articles:

1. How to Sell at Auction House. http://lauren-gallery.com/2017/06/19/how-to-sell-at-auction-house/

2. How to Buy at Auction House. http://lauren-gallery.com/2017/06/20/how-to-buy-at-auction-house/

3. How to Buy a House at Atlanta Auction House. http://lauren-gallery.com/2017/07/03/how-to-buy-a-house-at-atlanta-auction-house/

4. How to Sell a House at Georgia Auction House. http://lauren-gallery.com/2017/07/07/how-to-sell-a-house-at-georgia-auction-house/

5. How to Buy at Atlanta Fine Antiques. http://lauren-gallery.com/2017/07/07/how-to-buy-at-atlanta-fine-antiques/

6. Oberlo Review: Is Oberlo App Legit? http://lifeonearthasinheaven.blogspot.co.id/2017/05/oberlo-review-is-oberlo-app-legit.html

7. Do You Want to Be Number 1 on Google? Hire Richard Nata!
http://lifeonearthasinheaven.blogspot.co.id/2017/07/do-you-want-to-be-number-1-on-google.html

Thank you for your review.

Lord Jesus bless you.

Amen.

After several chats, the author gets the job.

You do not need to copy and paste the 3 examples above.

You'll have to change it to fit your persona.

You take the point of importance only, that is, if a boss asks A, then give him A+, then you will get a job from him/her.

Test Online

In fact, clients rarely ask you to do a test because your skills and ability can be assessed based on the portfolio you give. But there are also clients who ask you to test online first.

You are given time while taking the test online. So make sure your internet connection always good while taking a test.

Remember this!

Some clients will ask you to test by making an article or working on translating from language a into language b.

They will see the results of your work before they decide whether to use your services or not.

Be careful! Because they are deceiving you. They will deceive you with a variety of reasons because they will never want to pay you. Ha...7x

Interview through Chat, Email, or Video Call

Interviews are usually done via chat, email, or video call.

If you apply for a freelance job through the marketplace, you should communicate only through the message features that are there. Your data will be recorded so that if there is a dispute with the client, the data will be used as evidence to complete the arbitration.

Here is a list of often asked questions at the interview:

1. Can you tell me about yourself?

2. Why should we hire you? Why do you think you would be a good fit for the job?

3. Can you work together as a team?

4. What are you going to do with an annoying co-worker?

5. Is the money you asked for, can be deducted from X to Y?

6. Any questions you want to ask? Your client wants to hear you speak about what you already know about his/her company.

7. Etc.

Lessons Learned: What a Lost Test and/or Interview Really Tells You

If you fail in a test, then you should study harder when facing the next test at another client or company. If not, you can fail again in the face of the next test with another client or company.

If you fail in an interview, then you should practice harder when facing the next interview at another client or company. If not, you can fail again in the face of the next interview with another client or company.

Evaluate yourself. What causes you to fail during the test/interview. Then fix it.

You are on the right track if you experience rejection when you are applying for a freelance job.

Rejection doesn't mean you're bad or wrong – it means that you're learning and it's part of the process. In the beginning, you're probably not going to be great, but as time goes by, your skills, ability, knowledge, and portfolio will increase, and you will start to see results.

And if your next test/interview still fails, then evaluate and fix it again.

Always repeat the above method, until you get a freelance job from a client or company.

Why Didn't You Get a Freelance Job There?

The reasons you didn't get the freelance job there after testing and/or interview:

1. You are considered stupid for not being able to answer the questions given. You got a low score in test and/or interview.

2. Looks less convincing because you cannot or slowly answer one or more questions.

3. Caught lying.

4. Not polite.

5. Arrogant.

6. The price you are asking is too high. Usually, they will ask you to reduce your price.

7. There are other candidates who are better than you.

8. You are considered unsuitable to work with them.

9. Etc.

201 Amazing Ways to Make Your First $5,000 Faster

The list of jobs below will make you get $5,000 faster.

Through this book, the author will share 201 amazing ways to make your first $5,000 faster.

201 Jobs That Can Make Much Money:

1. Become a Writer.
2. Become a Freelance Writer.
3. Become an Author.
4. Become a Novelist.
5. Become a Ghostwriter.
6. Become a Blogger.
7. Become a Website Manager.
8. Become a Content Creator.
9. Become an SEO Writer.
10. Become a Business Plan Writer.
11. Become an Editor/Proofreader.
12. Become an Entrepreneur.
13. Become a Freelance Accountant.
14. Become a Notary Public.
15. Become a Freelance Bookkeeper.
16. Become a Freelance Auditor.
17. Become a Financial Analyst.
18. Become a Financial Planner.
19. Become a Retirement Planner.
20. Become a Small Business Consultant.
21. Become a Local Business Consultant.
22. Become a Tax Consultant.
23. Become a Business Advisor/Consultant.

24. Become a Public Speaker.
25. Become a Motivator.
26. Become a Private Teacher.
27. Become a Translator.
28. Become an Interpreter.
29. Become a Journalist/Reporter.
30. Become a Social Media Manager.
31. Online Marketing Specialist.
32. Being a Virtual Assistant or Personal Assistant.
33. Marketing Services in Social Media.
34. Become a Buzzer.
35. Become a Brand Ambassador.
36. Become a Web Site Developer.
37. Become a Website Administrator.
38. Become a Website Editor.
39. Become a Publisher.
40. Printing Business.
41. Become a Coach.
42. Personal Development Coach.
43. Create Online Courses.
44. Become a Public Speaker.
45. Become a Podcaster.
46. Become a Vlogger.
47. Become a Youtuber.
48. Become a Videographer.
49. Creating Video Clips.
50. Become an Influencer.
51. Become an Instagrammer.
52. Become an Entrepreneur or Solopreneur.
53. Become an Investor.
54. Become an Innovator.
55. Become a Nutritionist.
56. Become a Nurse.
57. Become a Nurse of Elderly.

58. Become a Nanny.
59. Become a Baby Sitter.
60. Become a Pet Sitter.
61. Become a Dog Trainer.
62. Become a Pet Grooming.
63. Become an Animal Breeder.
64. Become an Animal Care Services.
65. Become a Gardener.
66. Become a Celebrity.
67. Become an Entertainer.
68. Become a Master of Ceremonies (MC).
69. Become a Host.
70. Become an Event Organizer (EO).
71. Become a Songwriter.
72. Become a Boyband/Girlband.
73. Become a Band Manager.
74. Become a Cheerleader.
75. Become a Musician.
76. Become a Singer.
77. Become a Backing Vocal/Background Singer.
78. Become a Dancer.
79. Become a Choreographer.
80. Become a Dance Instructor.
81. Become a Fitness Instructor.
82. Become a Producer.
83. Become a Music Director.
84. Become a Film Director.
85. Become a Stuntman/Stuntwoman.
86. Become an Actor/Actress.
87. Become a Make-up Artist.
88. Become a Model.
89. Become a Modeling Agency.
90. Become an Advertising Agency.
91. Become a Comedian.

92. Become a Clown.
93. Become a Programmer.
94. Develop an App.
95. Become an Interior Designer.
96. Become a Graphic Designer.
97. Become a Jewelry Designer.
98. Become a Fashion Designer.
99. Become a Dressmaker.
100. Become a Taylor.
101. Become a Painter.
102. Become an Artwork Maker.
103. Become a Photographer.
104. Become an Art Photographer.
105. Become a Wedding Photographer.
106. Become a Wedding Organizer (EO).
107. Become a Bridal Consultant.
108. Become a Fashion Stylish.
109. Become a Hairdresser.
110. Become an Optician.
111. Become an Architect.
112. Become a Contractor.
113. Become a Promoter.
114. Become a Concert Promoter.
115. Become a Boxing Promoter.
116. Become a Personal Chef.
117. Culinary Business.
118. Become a Cake Maker.
119. Become a Tour Guide.
120. Become a Ticket Broker.
121. Become a Travel Agent.
122. Become a Trademark Agent.
123. Become an Agent/Distributor.
124. Become a Merchant.
125. Become a Social Worker.

126. Become a Sales Representative.
127. Become an Affiliate Marketing.
128. Become a Google Paid Ad Specialist.
129. Become a Fan Club Management.
130. Become an Athlete.
131. Become a First Aid/CPR Instructor.
132. Become a Detective.
133. Become a Counselor.
134. Become a Public Relations Consultant.
135. Become a Broker.
136. Become a Real Estate Broker.
137. Become a Lawyer.
138. Become a Pastor.
139. Become an Art Collector.
140. Become an Antique Dealer.
141. Become a Politician.
142. Become a Political Campaign Manager.
143. Become an Activist.
144. Become a Scientist.
145. Become a Lecturer.
146. Become a Train Driver.
147. Become an Online Driver.
148. Become a Barista.
149. Become a Waiter /waitress.
150. Become someone's friend. you can do this by joining a site like RentAFriend.
151. Become a Headhunter.
152. Become a Shopkeeper.
153. Souvenir Shop Business.
154. Mystery Shopper.
155. Car Washing Services.
156. Buying and Selling Cars.
157. Renting Your Car.
158. Sell the Secondhand Stuff.

159. Selling School Accessories.
160. Selling Football Equipment.
161. Selling Handmade Clothing and Garments.
162. Buy and Sell Websites
163. Buy and Sell Domain Names.
164. Become a Handicraft Maker.
165. Become a Dropshipper.
166. Online Retailer.
167. Online Shop.
168. Private Labeling.
169. DIY souvenirs.
170. Become a Typist.
171. Electronic Repair Service.
172. Courier Service.
173. Removal Service.
174. Repair Service.
175. Handyman work Service.
176. Engraving Service.
177. Gift Wrapping Services.
178. Laundry Service.
179. Home Decorating Service.
180. Cleaning Service.
181. Window Cleaning Service.
182. Carpet Cleaning Service.
183. Pool Cleaning Service.
184. Vacuum Cleaner Repair.
185. Telemarketing Service.
186. Newspaper Delivery Service.
187. Seminar Service.
188. Computer Maintenance Service.
189. Computer Training and Lessons.
190. Computer Repair.
191. A Mobile Auto Repair Business.

192. Rent out your home or your spare bedrooms. you can do this by joining the sites like Airbnb, Host or HomeAway.
193. Cash in on your skills or hobbies.
194. Become a Referee.
195. Become a Caddie.
196. Become a Scrapbooker.
197. Become a Paid Audience.
198. Become a Knitter.
199. Become an Embroider.
200. Participate in medical studies.
201. Sell your own products and/or services on the internet. Build an amazing product or service. The better product or service you build, the more income you'll receive.

In fact, there are still dozens or hundreds of other ways that are not the authors discussed in this book.

Why does not the author discuss it? Because 201 ways are too many, and you can choose only one or several jobs. Right? Ha...7x

Therefore, in this book, the author only discusses 50 amazing ways to make your first $5,000 faster.

Become a Writer

Being a writer is one of the most accessible jobs today. Since almost all large and small companies have one or several websites. And their website needs updating every day if they do not want their website to lose the visitors. Right?

Losing visitors may result in loss of revenue from advertising or selling of products and/or services from the company. Therefore, every day we can see tens of thousands of job openings looking for a writer in the world.

As a writer, you can choose to work full-time jobs in a company or full-time freelancer. Both can quickly generate $5,000 if you know the strategy.

The advantage of a writer is that you can have multiple professions at the same time.

An example is you are a writer. You can become a full-time freelancer, an author, a novelist, podcaster, vlogger, YouTuber, ghostwriter, writing coach, public speaker, and blogger too.

Here's a list of jobs for writers:

1. Become an Entrepreneur in the field of writing.

You could be a solopreneur or an entrepreneur.

A solopreneur if you do all the work alone.

An entrepreneur if you are helped by others in the works.

2. Become an Employee (Staff Writer) at the company.

3. Become a Staff Editor in the company.

4. Become a Freelance Writer.

The difference between a Solopreneur and a Freelance Writer.

A solopreneur is a self-employed Businessman. As an Entrepreneur, he/she has organized its operations into several divisions such as finance, marketing, and human resources. It's just that all the work of the various divisions done by himself/herself. Therefore, a solopreneur has already applied business principles in its work.

A Freelance Writer is a writer who works part-time without applying the principles in business.

5. Become an Author.

6. Become a Journalist, either for a magazine and/or newspaper. You can also become a Citizen Journalism.

7. Become a Playwright or Advertising Copy.

8. Become a Movie Script Writer.

9. Become a Script Editor.

10. Become a Novelist.

11. Become a Short Story Writer.

12. Become an Essayist.

13. Become an Article Writer.

14. Become a Copywriter.

15. Become a Creative Writer (screenplay, TV show).

16. Become a Ghostwriter.

17. Become a Content Writer or Content Creator in the website/blog.

18. Become a Slogan Writer.

19. Become a Writer who makes business planning (Business Plan Writer).

20. Become a Marketing staff.

21. Become a Translator.

22. Become a Website Admin.

23. Become a Social Media Manager.

24. Become an Audio Script.

25. Become a Columnist.

26. Become a Game Script.

27. Become a Grant Proposal Writer.

28. Become a Greeting Card Writer.

29. Become a Landing Page Writer.

30. Become a Commentary.

31. Become a Reviewer Products online.

32. Become a Presentation Script.

33. Become a User Manual Writer.

34. Become a Product Description Writer.

35. Become a Press Release Writer.

36. Become a Book Reviewer.

37. Become a Professional Beta Reader.

38. Become a Film /Movie Reviewer.

39. Become a Technical Writer.

40. Become a Tutorial online.

41. Become Travel Guides online.

42. Become a Biographer.

43. Become a Speechwriter.

44. Become a Poet.

45. Become a Lyricist.

46. Become a Proofreader.

47. Become a Virtual Assistant.

48. Become a Resume Writer.

49. Become a Travel Writer.

50. Become a Writing Coach.

51. Become a Literary Agent.

52. Become a How-to Book Writer.

53. Become an Annual Report Writer.

54. Become a Company Profile Writer.

55. Become a Content Strategist Writer.

56. Become a Librarian.

57. Become a Blogger.

58. Become a Podcaster.

59. Become an SEO Writer.

In this book, the author only discusses some professions from 59 professions that can be done by a writer above.

Become a Freelance Writer

How to become a freelance writer.
https://www.theguardian.com/.../how-become-freelance-writer-graduate-journalism

Get Paid to Write: How to Make Your First $100 as a Freelance Writer. https://thewritelife.com/how-to-make-your-first-100-as-a-freelance-writer/

If you love to write and feel the passion for writing, then you could be a writer. You can become a freelance writer. And as a freelance writer, then you can write articles, books/eBooks, essays, movies/book reviews, writing novels, etc.

And maybe this is your first step to becoming a famous author like Joanne Kathleen Rowling (J.K Rowling), Seth Godin, John Grisham, Agatha Christie, Enid Mary Blyton, etc.

It's actually very easy for you to earn money from writing. You write the articles. You make the 10 list or more of things you know, and then you send it to Listverse. To get further information at www.listverse.com /write-get-paid.

The question now is why you should send your article to Listverse? The answer is because of the requirements demanded by Listverse very easy, and the pay was good.

Listverse was built on the efforts of readers just like you. Readers who didn't have any experience as writers but decided to put a list together (1,500 words/10 items minimum), and send it in. If published, then you get $100.

You can start your career as a freelance writer to write an article for Listverse. If Listverse does not want to publish your article, do not despair. Try again and again, until your article published in Listverse. If you successfully publish your article in Listverse then make it as one of your portfolios as a freelance writer.

Before you send your articles then it is good to read and study the articles below.
a. 6 Reasons You Should Write For Listverse Today.
http://listverse.com/2014/02/18/top-6-reasons-you-should-write-for-listverse-today/
b. 10 Tips For Getting Paid To Write For Listverse.
http://listverse.com/2013/06/13/10-tips-for-getting-paid-to-write-for-listverse/
c. 10 Simple Steps To Get Your List Published On Listverse.
http://listverse.com/2015/05/24/10-simple-steps-to-get-your-list-published-on-listverse/

Of course, you can become a contributor or a Guest Poster on various other websites. But the authors recommend trying Listverse first. Because Listverse never asks clips of your articles as requested by other websites. :)

Besides Listverse, the Penny Hoarder also did not ask clips if you write to them. Just like Listverse, the Penny Hoarder also gave $100, if your article is published on the Penny Hoarder website.

Want a Freelance Writing Job? Get Paid to Write for The Penny Hoarder. https://www.thepennyhoarder.com/contributor-guidelines/

One advantage of the Penny Hoarder compared with Listverse is the payment system. You will receive extra money if you can get more readers.

Here's the breakdown:

When your post hits 50,000 pageviews, you earn $100.

When your post hits 100,000 pageviews, you earn another $200.

When your post hits 250,000 pageviews, you earn an additional $500.

The total possible bonus on each post is $800.

After **Listverse, The Penny Hoarder, you can try** Cracked. **because they do not ask for your portfolio.**

If you want to get paid better, then you should try writing for The Sun.

You can submit your article here.

https://www.thesunmagazine.org/submit.

https://www.thesunmagazine.org/news/submit-online-1.

The Sun pay you from $300 to $2,000 for essays and interviews, $300 to $1,500 for fiction, and $100 to $200 for poetry. **Very big money, isn't it? :)**

I hope someday my article published by The Sun so I get a lot of money. Ha...7x

In addition, you can find work in the writer's marketplace like Upwork, Freelancer, PeoplePerHour, ClearVoice, Izea, CloudPeeps, Express Writers, etc.

Remember this!

Your clients will not give you a better price for your service in the writer's marketplace just because you have a higher degree, but your skills, ability, knowledge, and portfolio make them pay better rates.

To win in the competition in the marketplace, you must make a great bid. In addition to the bid ways that the author has discussed before, you can also learn from the article below.

How to Become a Copywriter Quickly with No Experience, No Portfolio, and No Degree.
https://freelancetowin.com/how-to-become-a-copywriter/

Become an Author

An Author is a Writer who has published one or many books.

There are two types of authors, namely fiction and nonfiction.

Examples of nonfiction books are marketing books, recipe books, SEO books, Christianity books, etc.

An example of a fiction book is a novel. The author will be referred to as a novelist.

If your novel is good so you can make the movie version. And **someone to write the script** of the movie is called a Script Writer or Screenwriter.

Usually, an author specializes in his/her work. It will take the category of fiction or nonfiction. But you can write both if you have a talent for writing.

Writing a book is a lucrative investment. So write a book about your expertise. Then people will see you as an expert in the field you write. And it will help drive more revenue in the long-run.

Instead, take a moment to think about what motivates your readers.

Why do they buy books? Why do they buy YOUR books? What is it about YOU that appeals to them?

This is why you should create one or more books:

1. Your self-expression.

2. Build self-confident.

3. Become an agent of change.

4. Gain financial benefits.

5. Increase your knowledge.

6. Can make you more expert and professional.

7. Can make your name better known in the community.

8. Strengthen your memory.

9. Can make you become an open-minded person.

10. You will be respected by the readers of your book.

11. Have lots of fans.

12. Sharing your knowledge, theory, ideas, suggestions, criticism, opinion, or story into a book.

13. One way to brand yourself.

14. Invest in the future because you will get a passive income from the royalty.

15. Sometimes, if you're lucky, your book can help make your dreams come true.

16. Inner satisfaction. Proud of his/her own work.

17. It's a wonderful journey, and the satisfaction when you see your book in print is immense.

Top 8 Richest Authors in the World.
http://lifeonearthasinheaven.blogspot.com/2016/01/top-8-richest-authors-in-world.html.

Remember this!

Writing books is not a get rich quick scheme. But writing and publishing multiple books can be one of your smartest marketing strategies for long-term success. Why? You will be considered an expert in his field. After that, your credibility will always follow you wherever you go. Ha...7x

Many people think that being an author will make them rich. Though the fact is many authors whose lives are poor. Ha...7x

Why? Because you have to compete with millions of other authors in the world. And you lose the competition winning the hearts of the readers of the book.

Why are you not selling more books?

1. The title of your book does not attract people's attention.
2. The contents of your book are sad.
3. Cover your book pathetic.
4. The description of your book does not interest readers.
5. You chose the genre incorrectly. You choose a less buyer.
6. You choose the wrong topic. You choose a less buyer.
7. The selling price of your book is too expensive.
8. You don't promote enough. You can have the best story in the world, but if people don't know you exist, then you won't sell many copies or you sell nothing.
9. Many errors in typo, grammar, and spelling.
10. You do not have a book review or get a bad score on your book review.

If you want to be a rich author then there are four things you should do. First, sell your books. Second, create more books to sell your books more and more and more. Third, earn another income outside of selling books. For example, being a speaker at seminars or webinars, selling online courses, performing on various TV shows, etc. Fourth, make your books a testament to your knowledge, credibility, skills, ability, and experiences. After that, you can sell goods and/or services as your source of income.

- If you're a full-time author, you have to sell more books to keep doing what you're doing.

One way to sell more books is to copy and paste from authors who have proven successful in selling many more books. Of course, you cannot copy and paste 100% because you have to adjust to your book category.

Become a Novelist

Many people whose properties increased rapidly many times after they published one or several novels. The examples of some successful Novelist are J.K. Rowling, Stephen King, Agatha Christie, Enid Mary Blyton, Alfred Joseph Hitchcock, etc. Therefore, many people dream of becoming a Novelist.

In facts, there are tens of thousands to hundreds of thousands of novelists around the world whose books do not sell.

Factors that cause your book to sell poorly on the market:

1. Unattractive title.
2. Unattractive cover.
3. Cover that does not match the title.

4. Bad story.
5. Less promotion. So no one knows about your book.
6. Incorrect select categories and themes. You choose a less buyer.
7. Many errors in typo, grammar, and spelling.
8. The selling price of your book is too expensive.
9. Too many cliches.
10. The ending of the story is predictable.
11. You do not have a book review or get a bad score on your book review.
12. Etc.

Let's face it: writing a novel is hard unless you have a talent for writing, right?

So, if you do not have a talent for writing, then never make a novel. Because, if you push yourself to make a novel, then you can never finish it or the story of your novel ends up sad or not sold. Ha...7x

Do not be sad, for too long with the above facts because you can learn to write a novel via the internet. You can learn through articles, books, seminars, or courses provided by successful novelists.

You should know this!

The author will show one big secret from successful authors who are giving paid courses:

1. Some, even most of their income is earned from their paid courses. If the course price is $997 per person, then enough 100 participants, they already get money $99,700 deducted costs and fees (it is not large). If a paid course is done every month, then in one year, they get 12 x $99,700 = $1,196,400 deducted costs and fees.
2. Income above does not include royalties from their books sold on Amazon, bookstore, iBook, Kobo, or sold to course participants.
3. Income above does not include from the purchase of copyright to make a movie based on their novels.
4. Income above does not include honorarium when they are invited to various events, such as TV shows or seminars.
5. Therefore, do not be surprised if a famous author can get income 7-8 figure every year.

You can also get it all if you can make your book a Best Seller on Amazon or New York Time Best Seller.

Here's how to make your book sell more and more:

1. Set your goal.
2. Use many tools.

3. Read a good novel every day to expand the way you see everything.
4. Start reading a good novel and write your novel today.
5. Do some research before writing a novel.
6. Research on novels that become best sellers.
7. Research on novel titles that interest people to read your novel.
8. Set the keyword.
9. Start to promote your novel. If necessary, promote your novel before you start writing a single word of the contents of your novel.
10. Start to sell your novel. If necessary, sell your novel before you start writing a single word of the contents of your novel. You can sell your novel through your website or website from crowdfunding like [Kick Starter](), and [Indie Gogo](), and [Go Fund Me]().
11. Set an outline and plot.
12. Create the main character who struggles to make his/her dream.
13. Create another character who supports and opposes the struggle of the main character.
14. Start writing.
15. Write from the deepest heart.
16. Write daily to improve the skills of your writing techniques.

17. Set your BIC (Butt In the Chair) time every day.
18. Tracked your progress every week or month.
19. After the novel is finished, then editing and proofread the story path.
20. Research the agents, editors, and graphic designs for your book cover.
21. Then create a book cover that can sell.
22. Research the publishing houses before submitting your manuscript.
23. Send a query letter that demonstrates your professionalism.
24. You can pitch it like a pro.
25. Offer novel to the publisher or publish it yourself.
26. Promote your novel through social media to the world.
27. Create many guest posts about the topic similar to your book.
28. Instead, offer or give back something valuable in return. So make sure your book is really valuable to the targeted audience.
29. Build relationships with your audiences
30. Valuable content
31. Unique information
32. Maybe you doubt yourself sometimes, that's totally normal. But never give up.

If you do not have a talent for writing, then you should submit to a Ghostwriter to write your book.

Become a Ghostwriter

A Ghostwriter is a paid writer for writing articles, books, novels, essays, theses, etc.

If you become a ghostwriter, then the copyright of your work will be transferred to a third-party who pays you to write something. Instead, you will receive some money.

A ghostwriter rate with 5 or more years of work experience can reach $10,000 per manuscript. While a beginner's ghostwriter rate is only $500, it can even be offered for $250 per manuscript.
If your book or novel becomes a best-seller. Then your novel is making a movie script, then as a ghostwriter, you get nothing other than the money you have received. Because you have sold your manuscript and its copyright.
So you should consider once more, do you really want to be a ghostwriter?

Suggestions from the author, if you feel you have a talent for writing and people admit it, then you should not be a ghostwriter, but a freelance writer.

If you are looking for money, fame, and fortune, then you should not be a ghostwriter too.

Become a Blogger

Your talent for writing can also make you a blogger. You write articles that make people interested to read your articles. Then, tell friends and family about your articles. Then ask them to comment on your articles and share your articles with their friends and family. If you have many friends and your friends also have many friends then your articles will go viral quickly.

How to Blog: Blogging Tips for Beginners.
https://problogger.com/blogging-for-beginners-2/

40 Blogging Tips and Tricks for Beginners to Grow a Blog.
https://freshsparks.com/blogging-tips-and-tricks-for-beginners/

High Traffic Within 24 Hours.
http://lifeonearthasinheaven.blogspot.co.id/2017/10/high-traffic-within-24-hours.html

131 Tips to Increase Your Website/Blog Traffic Faster.
http://lifeonearthasinheaven.blogspot.co.id/2017/10/131-tips-to-increase-your-websiteblog.html

Writing for your blog has plenty of benefits.
1. Some people do it for fame.
2. Some do it for fortune.
3. Some do it for money.
4. Some do it for just do it.
5. Some do it for credibility.
6. Some do it for visibility.
7. Some even do it for fun!

If a lot of people come to visit your blog, then you have to write new articles, so that they stay loyal to your blog. If you have thousands of visitors each day so you can make places for ad space. Then you can offer the advertising ads so that you can earn passive income from blogging.

The way to get lots of visitors is to make your articles become viral.

How to make your articles become viral:

1. Create articles to educate the people.
2. Create the articles to entertain people.
3. Create the articles with emotionally engaged.
4. Create the articles by showing data and results.
5. Create the articles to make your readers happy.
6. Create the articles that can make your readers from curious to interested and become fans.
7. Create the controversial articles.
8. If you want your website to be viral then you should create the content that truly impacts your readers' lives.

After your articles become viral, you can register your blog to advertising companies such as Google Adsense, Chitika, Clicksor, AdFly, Yahoo! Publisher Network, Infolinks, BIDVertiser, Text-link-ads, Propellerads, Sitescout (formerly AdBrite), etc.

Or you just give the place where the advertising company can put advertisements on your website/blog. But you must have tons of visitors every day who read the articles on your website/blog, then they want to work with you.

In addition to the advertising, you can also earn money through affiliate marketing (affiliate-program amazon, ClickBank), reviewing products, sell your books/eBooks, write tutorials or guides, and became a Consultant.

Many successful bloggers are earning six or seven figures annually. So turn your blog into a freedom machine like them!

Here's a list of successful bloggers:
a. Jamie Frater owner of Listverse.
b. John Chow owner of http://johnchow.com.
c. Steve Pavlina owner of owner of http://stevepavlina.com.
c. Pat Flynn owner of SmartPassiveIncome.
d. Johnny Ward owner of OneStep4Ward.com.
e. Elsie Larson and Emma Chapman owner of A Beautiful Mess.
e. Arianna Huffington owner of The Huffington Post.
f. Timothy Sykes owner of http://timothysykes.com.
f. Michelle Schroeder-Gardner owner of Making Sense of Cents.
f. Kyle Taylor owner of The Penny Hoarder.
g. Michael Arrington owner of Techcrunch.
h. Jon Morrow owner of SmartBlogger (formerly boost blog traffic).
i. Vitaly Friedman owner of Smashing Magazine.
i. Pete Cashmore owner of Mashable.
j. Warren Rowse owner of Problogger and Digital Photography School.
k. Brian Clark owner of Copyblogger.
l. Neil Patel owner of KISSmetrics, Crazy Egg, and Hello Bar.

m. Chiara Ferragni **owner of** The Blonde Salad.
n. Heather Delaney Reese **owner of** It's a Lovely Life.

You're building your blog, working hard every day, hoping to one day your blog turn it into a full-time income, but you have no guarantees it will ever pay off.

What if you're wasting your time?

What if your blog does not earn a dollar after a few months?

What will you do next?

Remember this!

Many people dream of living comfortably after becoming a blogger. Few succeed but the most failed to achieve their dream.

If you want to succeed as a blogger then you have to sell products and/or services on your blog.

Do not expect income from ads like Google Adsense or affiliate marketing. Because to get a large income, then your blog must get hundreds of thousands to millions of visitors every month. Of course, it takes years to get thousands to millions of visitors every month. It may even be a lifetime, you can never get it.

Want More Traffic? 514 Tips to Skyrocket Your Website Traffic and Income Faster. https://www.amazon.com/dp/B0778LTNQ1.

How to Skyrocket 7-8 Figure Income Annually from Blogging. https://www.amazon.com/dp/B0765ZTCFX.

How to Create A Great Article for SEO in Three Hours.
https://www.amazon.com/dp/B01M0I6WMH.

Become a Website Manager

Many of the big blog owners do not have the time to take care of their website. Therefore, they pay a Website Manager to manage their blogs.

The tasks of a Website Manager are:

1. Search for one or several writers.

2. Search for one or more editors.

3. Publish articles after editing and proofreading by editors.

4. Search for advertisers on the website.

5. Promote new and old articles to make unique visitors more and more.

6. Keeping the Alexa website rank better and better.

7. Keeps the domain authority (DA) and page authority (PA) rankings of the website better.

Become a Content Creator

A Content Creator is a writer for one or more websites.

A Content Creator is responsible for creating articles or other content for a website to update content every day.

A large website usually has a lot of Content Creator.

The advantage of being a Content Creator:

1. If you become a Content Creator on a large website, then you will easily get a job when applying for work.

2. If you become a Content Creator on a large website, then you will easily win a bid when applying for a freelance job in the marketplace.

3. If you become a Content Creator on a large website, then your rate can go up.

4. If you become a Content Creator on a website, then your portfolio will become more worthy.

5. If you become a Content Creator on a website, then your value will grow bigger.

Become an SEO Writer

All websites are trying to get a spot on the first page of search engines. Not just websites, online stores, videos on YouTube, Facebook accounts, Instagram, Twitter, all trying to get a spot on the first page of search engines.

Fierce competition makes all websites that want to get a place on the first page of search engines, using SEO.

SEO is "search engine optimization."

An SEO Writer is an author who creates SEO articles.

If you managed to create a website for your client is on the first page of Google, then many website owners are willing to pay you high for their website can be on the first page of Google too.

If you can create a website for your client to be number 1 in Google, then your rate will be more expensive.

Why Google's first page? Because Google Chrome is the most used search engine in the world at the moment.

Become an Editor/Proofreader

If you are always careful, like to read and write. And you are proficient in one or more language, then you can become an editor or proofreader. Your task is to improve the writing of articles, books/eBooks, press releases, free from errors of typo, punctuation, grammar, spelling, and capitalization.

The more experienced you are as an editor and/or proofreader, the higher your rate.

Become an Entrepreneur

Become an entrepreneur is a gambler's profession. There is no guarantee of anything. You can put in a lot of time, a lot of effort, invest a great deal of emotional energy, and nothing may come out of it. There are no guarantees. So, unless one is fairly committed and willing to make that investment, don't do it.

Do you know what I mean? It takes a lot of energy.

When you understand what people are problems, what motivates them. Then you 're in a unique position to offer them what they want. And make them happy to pay for your products and/or services.

Congratulation! You are a successful entrepreneur if you really know some of the data above.

Is actually not hard to become an entrepreneur. Many of the people who started the business and they managed to become successful entrepreneurs. One recipe for starting a successful business is making your hobby as a business.

Here's a list of children who become successful entrepreneurs.
   a. Leanna Archer with her great-grandmother's secret recipe making and selling hair pomade to his family and neighbors. At that time, she was 9 years old. See her products at www.leannasinc.com.
   b. Robert Nay, a 14-year-old create the mobile game app called "Bubble Ball." Bubble Ball even beat the fame game "Angry Bird."
   c. 6-year-old Lizzie Marie Likness sell "Healthy Cooking." If you want to know the recipes then see at www.lizziemariecuisine.com.
   d. Etc.

If children can succeed in business then you can succeed in business too.

What You Can Learn From 8 Kids Already Making a Million Dollars. https://www.entrepreneur.com/article/241189

If you start a business from an early age, in the future it will be easier to get other ideas that could be used to run your business.

[4 Reasons WHY Your Kids Need to Learn Entrepreneurship (Even if They'll 'Have a Job')](https://domain.me/how-to-kids-entrepreneurship/). https://domain.me/how-to-kids-entrepreneurship/

Become a Business Plan Writer

Writing a business plan is not a guarantee of success, but can increase entrepreneurs' opportunities to succeed!

Remember this!

a. Some of the entrepreneurs need a business plan when they are starting a business.
b. Some of the entrepreneurs need a business plan when they are applying for a credit to the bank.
c. Some of the entrepreneurs need a business plan when they are looking for new investors to increase working capital from their company.

Why do some of the entrepreneurs need your help to write a business plan for their company?

1. They are busy so they don't have time to write their own business plan.

2. They cannot write a business plan for their company.

Become a Public Speaker

Did you know that you can get paid for your skill and/or life experiences?

Maybe you have had experiences in your life that made you stronger, made you more aware, or opened your audience's eyes to a new perspective.

Or do you have a life story to tell?

The world needs your message more than ever! Because it can change their lives. Now and forever.

The testimony of Steve Olsher: My highest paying speaking gig to date was $54,900 for an ONE HOUR talk!

Become a Motivator

The competition of life, the longer the harder. Problems come and go. The longer, the more people are stressed.

Many things that make people become stressed.

List of issues that make people stressful:

1. The life partner.

2. Girlfriend.

3. Family.

4. Finance.

5. Inflation and recession.

6. Debt.

7. Work.

8. Illness.

9. Others.

Stressed people often lose their zeal to do everything. As a result, they become increasingly stressed and depressed.

Depression that is too long makes many people commit suicide.

All that can be prevented if you can restore the spirit of life to them. How to motivate their lives to recover.

People who work to awaken the life spirits of others are named as a Motivator.

Of course, a Motivator is not only an uplifting life, but it also arouses morale among people who are stressed at work. Therefore, many big companies invite a famous motivator to raise the morale of employees. And employees who work spirit will generate greater profits for the company.

Become a Private Teacher

A good teacher can help people to understand new facts, ideas, and perspectives. So teaching is a transferable skill that you can use in lots of different formats and media.

You can try to offer giving extra lessons to students of primary or junior. For other subjects that could be taught and there is a variety such as math, physics, and foreign language which are usually the most difficult lessons according to many students. Offer your services become a private tutor to the parents of primary or junior, started from the nearest neighbor first.

Become an Online Teacher

You can offer courses online through your website.

You can offer courses online through a website like Udemy.

In addition to Udemy, you can teach online through Skillshare, Curious, Teachable, Teachlr, edureka !, Thinkific, Skillwise, OpenSesame, Coggno, Learning.ly, OfCourse, Simpliv, WizIQ, etc.

Perhaps you never thought about it before.

Or maybe you've already tried to get an online course going, but either didn't complete the project or didn't get many paying students.

That's fine. No matter how much (or little) course creation experience you have, I know a process that works - if you follow it.

So just do it.

Become a Translator

A business that is highly suitable for anyone who comprehends the language, whether it is English, Japanese language, the Dutch language, Mandarin, and other languages. Many people have started this side business because the business only needs language skills itself.

In addition to business purposes, a translator is also required to translate books, videos, movies, articles, essays, journals, etc.

Become an Interpreter

If you master both languages fluently, do not like nervous, and confident, then you can become an Interpreter.

You will be paid handsomely while translating directly from one language to another. Because you can help people overcome linguistic barriers and communicate effectively.

Many do not know that translating sign language goes into the Interpreter work category anyway. This profession is named as Sign language interpreters

Become a Journalist or Reporter

Almost all countries in the world have newspapers, magazines, and TV. Therefore, they need a lot of Journalists or reporters.

Apart from newspapers, magazines, and TV, some websites that provide online news also require a lot of Journalists or reporters.

Especially now, there is a profession as a Citizen Journalism. This job is a freelance job. So your income depends on your activeness in searching and writing news (articles).

Become a Nanny

This work is more suitable carried out by a girl or woman. For a job as a nanny, just keeping or caring for a child or several children who were left alone by their parents. Because if not accompanied by a Nanny, the child will feel lonely or afraid to be alone in the house. But it does not mean that this work can not be done by a man.

This is a part-time job because you only work until their parents return home. But if you advertise it will be a lot of people are looking for you to keep their children when they have to go.

There is no special skill to be a Nanny, but you should like children and can play with them. Because sometimes you will be asked to play with them.

Become a Baby Sitter

If there are a husband and wife who work to have a baby or toddler, then the wife should stop working to care for her children. Or they both ask for help from their parents to take care of their children. Or they give their children care to a third-party (Baby Sitter).

A Baby Sitter is usually a mother or a woman because women are more painstaking to care for babies or toddlers than men.

If you're younger than 14, you can't become a Baby Sitter.

If you become a Baby Sitter, then you are responsible for the food, drink, and health of the infant or toddler you care for.

You must be trained and have a certificate, then you can work as a Baby Sitter.

Become a Pet Sitter

There are so many people who have pets at home but don't have time to invite playing or feeding the animals. Whereas, if the animal is not maintained, of course, they would get sick and even die. Then you can become a pet sitter.

Your task as a pet sitter is very simple. You just feed the pets, washing clean the body, and invite to play. Moreover, you love pets, of course, is a very fun job. Besides, you can earn money on the job. Try to remember any of your friends or neighbors who have pets, then began to offer this service from now on.

Become a Dog Trainer

Requirements to become a Dog Trainer:

1. You have a dog or at least you have a dog.

2. You love to hang out and play with dogs.

3. You've trained your pet dog in some basic commands.

4. You've trained to be a Dog Trainer and have a certificate.

Become a Pet Grooming

The owners of dogs or cats race love to pamper their pets. They will dress and beautify their pets. The goal is to make the pet feel comfortable and beautiful so that it becomes healthier.

So the pets will be massaged, cut off their feathers, bathed, dressed, given good clothes, even given expensive jewelry.

For example, you can see in the movie "Beverly Hills Chihuahua."

Therefore, they like to groom their pets on a regular basis. Can be once a week or several times. At least once a month.

Of course, you have to learn and have a certificate, just be able to offer pet grooming services to society.

Become an Animal Breeder

Your job is to use your knowledge to protect a species or to select breeding stock that will produce superior offspring.

Not everyone can do this job, so you will be paying high if you can do it.

Animal Care Services

You can offer an animal care service.

The animal owners who are on vacation and cannot take their pets will leave it for you to be treated for several days or weeks.

Besides of that, you can offer aftercare for the pet in a convenient and affordable manner. So you can help the animal owners through this difficult time with their pets' aftercare.

You can offer to maintain the highest standards of cremation pet too.

Become a Gardener

If you like to plant and care for trees and flowers, then you fit with this job. Many people who have the flowers and garden but did not have enough time to take care of it. So if you can help take care of it, then they would give the money for your services.

Become an Entertainer

Being an entertainer means you must master one or more of these skills. You can sing, play music, or do stand-up comedy. You can also be a clown for children birthday party.

If you could be famous then you will get a thousand to tens of thousands $ every month. If you managed to become an entertainer on TV then you can get tens of thousands to millions of $ every month.

Become a Programmer

Programmer divided into the computer programmer, game programmer, developer, coder, or software engineer. To become a programmer, you must learn the language program. Here are some of the well-known programming language, COBOL, Fortran, Java, C#, VB, PHP, etc.

In the last decade, many students who are studying to become programmers. They can create their own program. They create programs of websites, templates, or games. If they can sell one or several of their programs so they will get a lot of money.

If you are a games programmer, then you can give your game for free as practiced by Rovio Entertainment with a game called Angry Birds. This game has been downloaded more than 1 billion times. They earn money from ads placed in gaming applications.

Or you can sell your game to the company.

Adam Hildreth set up the startup <u>Dubit Limited</u> at the age of 14 years old. If you're interested in kids digital entertainment, and you can make a good game for children, then you can join as their programmers.

Besides <u>Dubit Limited</u> Adam also founded <u>Crisp Thinking</u>, the company which protects brands from risks such as social media activist attacks and develops online child protection technology. Therefore do not be surprised if the wealth of Adam estimated net worth of £ 24 million ($40 million) in 2015, according to Sunday Times Rich List.

Chris Wanstrath and Preston-Werner founded GitHub based in San Francisco in 2008.

GitHub is the world's leading software development platform. It is a development platform inspired by the way you work. From open source to business, you can host and check code, manage projects, and build software along millions of other developers.

In 2018, Microsoft acquired GitHub for $7.5 billion.

Become a Fashion Designer

If you like the fashion and follow the development of the fashion world then you can try to become a fashion designer.

You can look for inspiration from fashion magazines and then you try to design your own fashion style.

You can make a nice and unique design. After that, you are wearing clothes the results of your own design. Then you can see how the reaction of your family and your friends. If they like your design, then you start offering your fashion design to your family and friends. If they are interested in buying then you can get the money and start your fashion business.

If you are lucky, then you can become famous like Donatella Versace, Christian Dior, Coco Chanel, Giorgio Armani, Donna Karan, **Oscar de la Renta**, Pierre Cardin, Calvin Klein, Ralph Lauren, etc.

Become a Graphic Designer

Many students have good skills in operating software such as Adobe Photoshop or CorelDRAW to make a graphic design.

Lots of people need graphic design services, especially those who like the design or art.

You can become a freelancer to solve their problems.

Show your design talent and offer design services to them. Suppose that the task of graphic design from friends, t-shirt design services, photo editing services, and other design services.

Here's a list of websites that give job board for programmers and graphic designers:
a. Awesomeweb. https://www.awesomeweb.com/
b. Krop. http://www.krop.com/
c. The Creative Group. http://www.roberthalf.com/creativegroup.

Christian Owens founded the design company at the age of 14 years old and at age 16, he got his first one million with Mac Bundle Box, a software promotion company which offers a bundle of Mac OS X applications at cut-rate prices but for a limited amount of time.

Become a Jewelry Designer

If you like the world of fashion and like the design, try to become a designer especially jewelry design.

As an extra point and distinguish you from the other stores, try to offer customized designs to your customers.

Find out what they like and design what they want. Then create a new design that describes the customer desires.

In the manufacture of jewelry, try to cooperate with local shops or jeweler in your town. If you have enough money, then develop the business by renting space and equipped with an adequate equipment.

Become a Painter

If you like to paint and feel have the talent to paint, then it is good to start a career as a painter.

You can create a website or blog and sell your paintings there.

You can also offer your paintings for sale via the websites below:
a. Veer. http://www.veer.com,
b. National Careers Service. https://nationalcareersservice.direct.gov.uk/advice/planning/jobprofiles/Pages/painteranddecorator.aspx
c. Artprice. http://www.artprice.com/

If you are well-known as a painter of the world then your works will enter the auction house Christie's. And you can sell your painting for hundreds of millions of $ there.

Top 5 most expensive paintings ever sold in history. http://lifeonearthasinheaven.blogspot.com/2015/11/top-5-most-expensive-paintings-ever.html.

Become a Photographer

These businesses are usually associated with the hobby. Of course, if your hobby could become a business then it would be very nice, isn't it?

An example of the hobby that can earn money is photography.

Many people want to get the best photo is, then stored on the laptop or published on their social media accounts. Of course, the business has a great potential if done well and has good management.

You can shoot anything, from your family, your dog, your friends, when you climb a mountain, go to the beach, and others. Your photos can sell through your website/blog or another website.

You can also offer your photos for sale via the websites below:
a. http://www.photos.com/
b. http://www.stockxpert.com/
c. http://www.istockphoto.com/

d. http://www.clipart.com/en/
e. https://submit.shutterstock.com/
f. Fotolia. https://www.fotolia.com/Info/Contributors.
g. Bigstock. http://www.bigstockphoto.com/sell-your-images.html
h. Alamy. http://www.alamy.com/contributor/
I. http://www.crestock.com/

They sell the photos to writers/journalists/media/magazines/newspapers which need photos as an illustration of their writing.

If you do not know how to sell your photos then read this guide.

How To Successfully Sell Your Photos Online As A Photographer.
https://graphpaperpress.com/blog/sell-photos-online/

What It Takes to Make $500 per Month Selling Stock Photos.
https://www.makeuseof.com/tag/make-money-selling-stock-photos/

Become an Art Photographer

Photography is a profession that appeals to many people. Especially after the price of digital cameras become cheaper. This makes everyone become a Photographer, right? It is fun, interesting, and has various facets to it.

As an Art Photographer, you will produce photos with themes and concepts that include elements that contain mood and emotion. The goal is to dramatize the atmosphere and arouse the mood and emotions of the audiences.

If your photo is good, then many people are willing to pay high for your artwork.

Become a Wedding Photographer.

A wedding is a sacred moment for both brides. Therefore, they are willing to pay high your skills and experiences, to capture the moment in the form of several photo albums and video.

You should be able to edit photos and/or video, so you can give the maximum results.

If your result is good, then many people are willing to pay high for this job.

Become a Freelance Cameraman

This profession is needed by many people because:

1. People need the video making at their family weddings.

2. Officials need the making of videos in various activities, especially their social activities.

3. The school requires the making of the video in the annual graduation ceremony.

4. TV requires documentation in the video when covering an event or news.

5. A professional Cameraman is required in the making of a documentary film.

6. A professional YouTuber requires a professional Cameraman when creating the contents for them making money.

Become a YouTuber

Open an account on YouTube. Create a channel on your YouTube account. Enable your channel for monetization. Connect your **YouTube** channel to an AdSense account to **earn money** and get paid for your monetized videos.

Make one or several videos. Make the unique video, interesting, and nice that people want to watch. Create an attractive headline so that people feel curious to watch. Then upload the video to YouTube.

Then building your subscribers. The more subscribers, the better.

Then promote these videos to all people around the world. If hundreds of thousands or millions of people watching your video, then you will get big money.

Your earning = CPM x (total impression/1000).

CPM is *Cost per Mille.*

1000 views = $1.

10.000 views = $10.

100.000 views = $100.

1.000.000 views = $1000.

10.000.000 views = $10,000.

100.000.000 views = $100,000.

1,000.000.000 views = $1,000,000.

Each country has a different rate. For countries that use English as a native language, the CPM is higher than those that do not.

You can make videos that discuss anything on YouTube. But the most viewers on YouTube are music videos.

Here's a list of people who are successful in YouTube:
a. **PSY – Gangnam Style**. This video got more than 3.1 billion views.
b. **Taylor Swift – Blank Space**. This video got more than 2.3 billion views.
c. **Justin Bieber – Baby**. This video got more than 1.9 billion views.
d. Katy Perry – Roar. This video got more than 2.5 billion views.
e. Meghan Trainor – All About That Bass. This video got more than 2.2 billion views.

Here's a list of kids who are successful in YouTube:
a. Evan – EvanTubeHD.
b. Mya – Full-Time Kid.
c. Yebin – Baby Yebin.
d. James Hashimoto – Action Movie Kid.

Creating Video Services

Currently, many tools make your video production easier.

The easiest video tools for you:

1. Animoto. https://animoto.com/
2. Distill. www.wedistill.io/
3. iMovie app. https://www.apple.com/id/imovie/
4. Nutshell. https://itunes.apple.com/us/app/nutshell-camera-instant-mini-movies-text-animation/id953435157?mt=8.
5. Magisto. https://www.magisto.com/
6. Pexels Videos. https://videos.pexels.com/
7. Videoshop. https://videoshop.net/
8. YouTube Audio Library. https://www.youtube.com/audiolibrary/music?feature=blog.

So you can start today. Create your offer and start looking for the clients. Ha...7x

Make Video Subtitling

There are thousands of languages in the world. And most people only understand one, two, or several languages only. So if they want to understand a movie, video, or game from abroad, they need to translate the foreign languages into their language.

A movie, video, or game will be sold more if subtitled. Because people will understand the way the story they watch or plays after giving the subtitle.

There are three conditions needed to create a video subtitling:

1. Fluent in two or more languages.

2. Have tools that help in make video subtitling.

3. An expert in using the tools above.

10 Free Useful Subtitle Maker Tools:

1. Aegisub Advanced Subtitle Editor. www.aegisub.org/
2. AHD Subtitles Maker. https://sourceforge.net/projects/ahdsubtitles/
3. DivXLand Media Subtitler. https://divxland-media-subtitler.en.lo4d.com/
4. SubtitleCreator. subtitlecreator.sourceforge.net/
5. SubEdit Player. http://www.free-codecs.com/download/subedit_player.htm.
6. Subtitle Edit. http://www.digital-digest.com/software/Subtitle_Edit.html.
7. Subtitle Workshop. subworkshop.sourceforge.net/download.php.
8. VisualSubSync. https://www.videohelp.com/software/VisualSubSync.
9. WinSubMux. https://www.videohelp.com/software/WinSubMux.

Make Video/Audio Transcript

A Reporter, Journalist, or Blogger sometimes interviews someone. The result of the interview is recorded on audio/video.

Interview results should be transcribed into writing to be read by the audience. Therefore, you can offer services to create a video/audio transcript to them.

Gift Wrapping Services

Everyone certainly has a birthday. At birthdays, generally, family and closest friends will give a congratulatory gift on the birthday.

A good chance for you to try to create a gift wrap service business which unique and different from the others. This effort is relatively easy.

Simply buy some wrapping paper as well as having a unique quality, and several scissors and decorations for the gifts. Then, offer these services through the school wall magazines or your classmates. The more unique your gift wrapping creations, certainly more and more people interested in.

Sell the Secondhand Stuff

The next sideline business for people is selling second-hand goods. The goods you sell are goods used but still in good condition. An example is a laptop, a smartphone, etc.

In fact, this item could be the worthy goods if we marketed to people who really need it. You wholesale goods at flea markets, then you resell to your friends in your community. Or you sell via online.

Online Shop

This is the business that is most preferred by people. How to start this business is very easy. Doesn't necessarily need anything capital, just a smartphone, and an internet connection.

You can create your own shop through your website or blog. Or you can also open your store in the marketplace like Amazon, eBay, Clickbank, etc.

After that, you can open your shop. You have to find another way or a special product that interested customers to visit your online shop and shopping at your place.

Sell products that pay you over and over.

Culinary Business

For you in particular who have a hobby of cooking, you can use cooking skills for a culinary business.

The business can be started by selling in the school canteen, just a simple menu that is not too takes up much of your time in making it. Such as drinks business, snacks, and the others. You can also start your culinary business from home.

Become a Virtual Assistant

You can offer services to be a Virtual Assistant.

Many people do not have the time to do some tasks so they need help from you.

Examples of work from a Virtual Assistant are:

1. Data entry.
2. Online research.
3. Researching/making travel and accommodation arrangements.
4. Bookkeeping.
5. Typing.
6. Personal duties, like paying bills, buying gifts, dry cleaning, booking restaurants and events, house moving, researching cheaper utility companies, etc.
7. Forum /blog commenting.
8. Facebook, Twitter, or Google ads – creating, monitoring and analyzing.

9. Designing/formatting infographics, logos, banners, social media profile images.
10. Transcription.
11. Etc.

Marketing Services in Social Media

Many entrepreneurs who have accounts on various social media. They do not have time to take care of their accounts. If they hire an employee to take care of their accounts that are very expensive. So they are looking for a person who can manage their accounts on various social media.

This is an opportunity for you to work part-time. Offer your services to small-scale businesses to become the administrator on their Instagram, Twitter, and Facebook account.

Through the social media, you can also run marketing services. Of course, you must be an expert in marketing, then you can run this business. So you must read and learn the guide marketing plan and marketing strategy.

Become a Buzzer

If you are an influencer, famous, or have tens of thousands to millions of followers on social media, then you can make money by becoming a Buzzer.

Many brands that are willing to pay you high if you want to endorse their products.

Not only brands, politicians also dare to pay you high to influence the people to choose them in the election of Mayor, Governor, Senator, or President.

DIY souvenirs

If you do not spend a lot of time hanging out or lazing in bed then you have a lot of spare time. You can use it to make souvenirs like "Do It Yourself (DIY)."

To start this business then, you have to learn to make souvenirs. You can look for inspiration from newspapers, magazines, the Internet, or other places. Begin to offer a lot of souvenirs to friends, family, or relatives who are making birthday parties or other family events.

Become a Singer

Become a Singer If you like singing and your voice is good, then you can Become a Singer. Currently a lot of singing contest on TV shows.

You can get there to register as a contestant. Then practice your vocal voice.

Invite your family, friends, neighbors, and all the people you know to support you during the preliminary round.

If you get away from the preliminary round, then ask your family, friends, neighbors, and all the people you know to invite their families, friends, neighbors, and all the people their know to support you as long as you are still in the race.

You can also upload videos while you are singing on YouTube. If your video becomes viral and is seen by tens of millions of people, there will be labels that invite you to record and make an album with them.

That's what Justin Bieber did before he got a record contract from a label.

Bieber's current manager, Scooter Braun first discovered him through his YouTube video in 2007. Scooter was impressed with his video and contacted Pattie Mallette, Justin's mother about the desire to work with him. After convincing his mother, Braun arranged for Justin to meet Usher in Atlanta, Georgia. Then Justin signed a contract with RBMG, and then Justin goes to Island Records because of the contract offered by recording executives, LA Reid.

In this book, the author only discusses some professions from 50 professions that can make your first $5,000 faster.

Conclusion

To be successful requires hard work and success cannot be achieved overnight. Successful businesses sacrifice a lot of time. Only hard work can grow your business.

Based on the various information described above, we can conclude as follows:
1. Determine your career goals as a full-time freelancer.
2. The younger you start looking for money, then the faster you can succeed in the future.
3. If you fail, then do not give up. Learn more and develop your skills, ability, and knowledge. Try and try again, until you get it.

4. Looking for real money is easy, as long as you are willing to work hard and use the best of your ability, skills, knowledge, and experiences.
5. Your hobby can become your business.
6. Social media allow us to create a business.
7. Prayer and work (ora et labora). Do not worry. Believe with all your heart.

"Have not I commanded thee? Be strong and of a good courage; be not afraid, neither be thou dismayed: for the LORD thy God [is] with thee whithersoever thou goest (Joshua 1:9)."

If you can make your first $5,000 yourself, then you do not need to ask for money from your parents. So what are you waiting for? Start making money today! And make your parents proud of you. :)

So, what are you waiting for? Are you going to focus on building a full-time freelance career?

It's your time to get money!

Stop dreaming and start action to **Make Your First $5,000 Faster.**

Don't waste any more time! Start action now.

www.ingramcontent.com/pod-product-compliance
Lightning Source LLC
Chambersburg PA
CBHW030702220526
45463CB00005B/1862